Worksheets
Don't Grow Dendrites

Marcia L. Tate

Worksheets
Don't Grow Dendrites
20 Instructional Strategies That Engage the Brain

CORWIN PRESS, INC.
A Sage Publications Company
Thousand Oaks, California

For information:

Corwin Press, Inc.
A Sage Publications Company
2455 Teller Road
Thousand Oaks, California 91320
www.corwinpress.com

Sage Publications Ltd.
6 Bonhill Street
London EC2A 4PU
United Kingdom

Sage Publications India Pvt. Ltd.
B-42 Panchsheel Enclave
Post Box 4109
New Delhi 110 017 India

Printed in the United States of America

Library of Congress Cataloging-in-Publication Data

Tate, Marcia L.
Worksheets don't grow dendrites: 20 instructional strategies
that engage the brain / Marcia L. Tate.
        p. cm.
Includes bibliographical references and index.
ISBN 0-7619-3880-X-ISBN 0-7619-3881-8 (pbk.)
   1. Effective teaching-Handbooks, manuals, etc. 2. Lesson planning-Handbooks,
manuals, etc. 3. Learning. I. Title.
LB1025.3 .T29 2003
371.3´028—dc21

                                        2002154030

03   04   05   06   10   9   8   7   6   5   4   3   2   1

Acquisitions Editor:	Rachel Livsey
Editorial Assistant:	Phyllis Cappello
Production Editor:	Melanie Birdsall
Copy Editor:	Toni Williams
Typesetter:	C&M Digitals (P) Ltd.
Indexer:	Michael Ferreira
Proofreader:	Desiree Dreeuws
Cover Designer:	Tracy E. Miller
Production Artist:	Lisa Miller

Contents

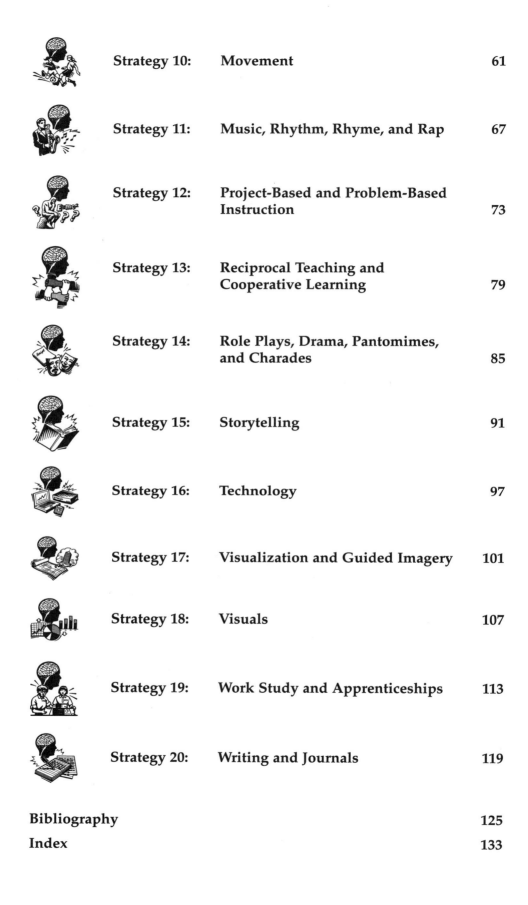

Figure 1.1 Mrs. Dozier's classroom

Introduction
Worksheets
Don't Grow Dendrites

20 Instructional Strategies That Really Work!

Allow me to tell you a story. Visualize the following classrooms, if you will.

Mrs. Dozier teaches 11th grade British literature at George Washington High School. Lecture is her primary method of delivering instruction. Sometimes the lectures last for more than half the period. Today the lecture is about the Shakespearean play, *Romeo and Juliet.* Some of the higher achieving students are paying close attention since they know that much of the information will appear on the midterm exam. Other students are maintaining eye contact with Mrs. Dozier while thinking about everything except the play. Several students are engaged in conversation and are promptly reprimanded. Mrs. Dozier doesn't realize that most of the class stopped listening to her lectures during the first few weeks of school. A few have retained enough information from the lectures to regurgitate it on the multiple-choice, teacher-made test, but, if asked, will admit that they do not really understand Shakespeare's work any better now than before the lectures began (see Figure 1.1).

Mr. Pope teaches the same course at Southwest High School. He is the favorite teacher of most of the students in his class. He has very few, if any, behavior problems. Mr. Pope must cover the same curriculum as Mrs. Dozier; however, the two classrooms bear little resemblance to one another. Mr. Pope is also teaching *Romeo and Juliet.* Last week, he completed a graphic organizer on the board that accompanied his seven-minute minilecture, pointing out the traits of several of the main characters. Mr. Pope's students also began working in cooperative groups to rewrite five different scenes from the play into dramatic presentations. Students have been assigned parts and today they will dramatize the scenes previously written. Students will grade one another's presentations according to a rubric they helped develop (see Figure 1.2).

Figure 1.2   Mr. Pope's classroom

WHY THESE STRATEGIES?   ■

Which teacher would you rather have? Which teacher would you rather be? With former president George Bush having declared the 1990s the Decade of the Brain, millions of dollars have been spent on brain research. As a result, teachers, as growers of brain cells, ought to know more today about how students learn than ever in the history of the world. Much of this recent knowledge has come from consultants such as Eric Jensen (1995, 2000, 2001), David Sousa (2001), Robert Sylwester (1995), and Patricia Wolfe (2001), who make practical application for educators from the research of the neuroscientists.

While caution against making immediate application of the neuroscientists' findings is certainly in order, teaching and learning cannot wait. Exemplary teachers have always known that active engagement of students is not a luxury but a necessity if students are to truly acquire and retain content, not only for tests, but for life.

Learning style theories that call for student engagement have been proposed for decades, as evidenced by the copyright dates of some research. Whether you are examining Bernice McCarthy's 4MAT Model (1990), Howard Gardner's theory of multiple intelligences (1983), or VAKT (visual, auditory, kinesthetic, tactile) learning style theories, similar instructional delivery systems appear to consistently emerge. In addition, because of modern technological advances such as PET scans, CAT scans, and fMRIs (functional magnetic resonance imaging), neuroscientists now appear able to identify physiological reasons for why some instructional strategies simply engage the brain better than others. That is why most *Worksheets Don't Grow Dendrites!*

TATE'S 20   ■

I have identified 20 strategies that, according to brain research and learning style theory, appear to correlate with the way the brain learns best. In my 28 years in education, I have observed hundreds of teachers—regular education, special education, and gifted as well. Regardless of the classification or grade level of the student or the content area of the instructor, exemplary teachers consistently use these 20 strategies to deliver memorable classroom instruction and help their students understand and retain vast amounts of content.

This book will attempt to accomplish three things:

- Identify and describe each of the 20 brain-compatible strategies;

- Provide over 200 research rationales as to why these strategies appear to take advantage of the way the brain learns best;

- Supply over 150 examples of ways in which these strategies can be used to ensure that students are mastering curricular objectives and meeting national standards.

Comparison of Tate's 20 Instructional Strategies to Learning Theory		
Tate's 20	*Multiple Intelligences*	*VAKT*
Brainstorming and discussion	Verbal-linguistic	Auditory
Drawing and artwork	Spatial	Kinesthetic/tactile
Field trips	Naturalist	Kinesthetic/tactile
Games	Interpersonal	Kinesthetic/tactile
Graphic organizers, semantic maps, and word webs	Logical-mathematical/ spatial	Visual/tactile
Humor	Verbal-linguistic	Auditory
Manipulatives, experiments, labs, and models	Logical-mathematical	Tactile
Metaphors, analogies, and similes	Spatial	Visual/auditory
Mnemonic devices	Musical-rhythmic	Visual/auditory
Movement	Bodily-kinesthetic	Kinesthetic
Music, rhythm, rhyme, and rap	Musical-rhythmic	Auditory
Project-based and problem-based instruction	Logical-mathematical	Visual/tactile
Reciprocal teaching and cooperative learning	Verbal-linguistic	Auditory
Role plays, drama, pantomimes, charades	Bodily-kinesthetic	Kinesthetic
Storytelling	Verbal-linguistic	Auditory
Technology	Spatial	Visual/tactile
Visualization and guided imagery	Spatial	Visual
Visuals	Spatial	Visual
Work study and apprenticeships	Interpersonal	Kinesthetic
Writing and journals	Intrapersonal	Visual/tactile

The examples provided in this book are just that, examples. Once you get a feel for how to apply each strategy, you will be able to create your own activities with ease. That is why the last part of each chapter asks you to reflect on the application of the strategy for your own specific objectives and classroom instructional practice.

Watch the difference in the motivation, energy level, and, most important, academic achievement of your students when these strategies are appropriately and consistently used. Teaching any other way is not very memorable, and, by the way, just plain boring. So, have fun with this book, and enjoy the strategies. After all, the use of humor is one of the 20!

Acknowledgments

It is my belief that every student comes with an inherent gift, a package, so to speak. It is the job of an educator to unwrap this gift to find the most viable means by which each student can excel. As society has changed, so has the packaging, necessitating the need for alternative ways of unwrapping these packages.

My gratitude goes to those educational consultants who are giving us additional ways to unwrap these gifts by translating the findings of the neuroscientists into educational practice and to those teachers who use interactive strategies to engage the brains of their students.

Speaking of gifts, I am deeply grateful for family members and professional educators who have supported me through and assisted me with this endeavor. To my husband and best friend, Tyrone, whose steadfast belief and constant encouragement enable me to unwrap each day with enthusiasm and a belief that all things are possible.

To my dear children—Jennifer, Jessica, and Christopher. I write this book as much for them as for anyone since their learning styles are as different as their personalities. Teachers can always unwrap Jenny's gifts by involving her in hands-on activities. Jessie can always adapt her gifts to the instruction provided. Chris, on the other hand, has to be bodily engaged in the task at hand. He has to draw and build and act, and drum, and sing. Therefore, unless his teachers use these strategies, school is not his favorite place to be. I dedicate Tate's 20 strategies to them and to other students just like them.

To the DeKalb County Professional Development Department and especially Joy Ross, whose technical expertise has always made me look good. Working with the department to improve instruction daily is truly a present.

The contributions of the following reviewers are gratefully acknowledged:

Donna Walker, Ed.D.
Consultant
Strategic Teaching and Learning L.L.C.
Dallas, TX

About the Author

 **Marcia L. Tate**, Ed.D., is the Executive Director of Professional Development for the DeKalb County School System, Decatur, Georgia. During her 28-year career with the district, she has been a classroom teacher, reading specialist, language arts coordinator, and staff development director. Dr. Tate received the 2001 Distinguished Staff Developer Award for the State of Georgia and her department was chosen to receive the 2002 Exemplary Program Award for the state.

She is also an educational consultant and has presented to over 50,000 administrators, teachers, parents, and business and community leaders throughout the United States. She is a member of the National Speaker's Bureau for the Teacher's Workshop and has presented at numerous state, national, and international conferences. Her workshops receive rave reviews since she uses the strategies in this book to engage adult brains as she presents. In March 2002, she was featured in a national teleconference, *Brain-friendly Reading,* along with Carolyn Chapman.

She holds a bachelor's degree in psychology and elementary education from Spelman College, a master of arts degree in remedial reading from the University of Michigan, an educational specialist degree from Georgia State University, and a doctorate in educational leadership from Clark Atlanta University. Spelman College awarded her the 1994 Apple Award for excellence in the field of education.

Marcia can be contacted by calling (770) 465-4017 or by email: marciata@bellsouth.net. Visit her website at www.developingmindsinc.com.

Strategy 1

Brainstorming and Discussion

WHAT: DEFINING THE STRATEGY

The brain is a highly social organism. If you don't believe that statement, just arrive early at a faculty meeting or any other type of social gathering, particularly one where people know one another. Watch what happens as people begin to arrive. Most of them take the opportunity to converse with one another. Very few, if any, sit in silence.

Then visit a traditional classroom where students spend most of their time engaged in individual activity without the benefit of conversation and, in fact, are expected to sit in silence for a greater period of the day. What is wrong with this picture? Perhaps teachers are expecting students to exhibit behavior that is unnatural to the brain. You see, discussion has many advantages, not the least of which is that simply opening the mouth to speak sends oxygen to the brain and facilitates dendritic growth.

When students are given the opportunity to brainstorm ideas without criticism, to discuss opinions, to debate controversial issues, and to answer questions at all levels of Bloom's taxonomy, wonderful things can happen that naturally improve comprehension and higher order thinking.

HOW: SAMPLE CLASSROOM ACTIVITIES

- Level/Subject Area: Elementary/Middle/High (Cross-curricular)

  Standard/Objective: Encourage divergent thinking.

  Activity: Students are given a question to which there is more than one appropriate answer. Students brainstorm as many ideas as

1

WHY: RESEARCH RATIONALE

Students learn 90% of what they say or discuss as they complete an activity. (Dale, 1969)

Learner performance scores improved when learners were asked questions of greater depth. (Redfield & Rousseau, 1981)

Better quality questions result in more challenge to the thought processes of the brain. (Berliner, 1984)

Learning increases when students have the opportunity to talk about it in their own words; to make it their own. (U.S. Department of Education, 1986)

Students who discuss how they and others think become better learners. (Astington, 1998)

Regardless of the topic or task, small-group discussion reinforces classroom learning, assists the brain in recalling the information, and allows students to solve problems collaboratively and explore topics in depth. (Alexopoulou & Driver, 1996)

The ability to ask questions allows individuals to be creative, to imagine beyond what is given, to search for missing information, physical rationales, and human purposes that will explain the given. (Harpaz & Lefstein, 2000)

It is unrealistic for teachers to formulate questions for students since, in real life, students are required to form their own questions. (Sternberg & Grigorenko, 2000)

When students generate their own questions, they become actively engaged in reading and motivated by their own queries rather than those of the teacher. (Report of the National Reading Panel, 2000)

The process of brainstorming can be used to activate prior knowledge since one student's idea causes other students to scan their neural networks for related ideas. (Gregory & Chapman, 2002)

possible in a designated time period using the DOVE guidelines: Defer judgment, One idea at a time, Variety of ideas, and Energy on task.

- Level/Subject Area: Elementary/Middle/High (Cross-curricular)

  Standard/Objective: Increase higher order thinking skills.

Activity: Students answer content-related questions at all levels of Bloom's taxonomy using the question stems provided below. Include all levels of questioning in discussion groups as well as on teacher-made tests.

- Level/Subject Area: Elementary/Middle/High (Language Arts/History)

  Standard/Objective: Increase higher order thinking skills.

  Activity: Students discuss how they would react if they found themselves in the same situation as a literary character or a historical figure. Example: What would you have done if you found yourself alone in the wilderness for an extended period of time, as Brian did in the story *Hatchet*, by Gary Paulsen?

- Level/Subject Area: Elementary/Middle/High (Mathematics)

  Standard/Objective: Solve a math problem.

  Activity: Students are given a math problem to solve. Ask each student in a group to describe how a solution was reached. When all have finished, students' varying paths to the answer are compared and discussed, allowing them to see that there may be more than one way to solve a problem.

- Level/Subject Area: Elementary (Science/Mathematics)

  Standard/Objective: Comprehend the term *ratio*.

  Activity: Show the class a can of frozen juice and ask students if they have ever mixed juice using a concentrate. Ask them to explain the procedure of blending three cans of water to one can of concentrate (a ratio of three parts water to one part concentrate). Students then brainstorm additional examples of ratios from their own experiences.

- Level/Subject Area: Elementary/Middle/High (Cross-curricular)

Standard/Objective:	Read a variety of texts.
Activity:	Students form interest groups and each group selects and reads a text or book of interest. Students then meet to discuss the text by asking questions of one another, making connections, and challenging one another's opinions.

- Level/Subject Area: Elementary/Middle/High (Cross-curricular)

Standard/Objective:	Read a variety of texts.
Activity:	Students peruse books, magazines, newspapers, or the Internet to find information that is of interest to them. Students focus on the pertinent points, ask questions, and provide their personal insights on the information. They then present a summary of the information to the class. Classmates ask original questions using the question stems provided below.

Model Questions and Key Words to Use in Developing Questions

I. **Knowledge** (eliciting factual answers, testing recall and recognition)

Who	Describe
What	Define
Why	Match
When	Select
Where	Which one
How	What is the one best
How much	Choose
What does it mean	Omit

II. **Comprehension** (translating, interpreting, and extrapolating)

State in your own words	Summarize
What does this mean	Select

Give an example

Condense this paragraph

State in one word

What part doesn't fit

What restrictions
 would you add

What exceptions are there

Which is more probable

What are they saying

What seems to be

What seems likely

Classify

Judge

Infer

Show

Indicate

Tell

Translate

Outline

Match

Explain

Represent

Demonstrate

Which are facts, opinions

Is this the same as

Select the best definition

What would happen if

Explain what is happening

Explain what is meant

Read the graph, table

This represents

Is it valid that

Which statements support the
 main idea

Sing this song

Show in a graph, table

III. Application (to situations that are new, unfamiliar, or have a new slant for students)

Predict what would happen if

Choose the best statements that apply

Select

Judge the effects

What would result

Explain

Identify the results of

Tell what would happen

Tell how, when, where, why

Tell how much change there would be

IV. Analysis (breaking down into parts, forms)

Distinguish

Identify

What assumptions

What motive is there

What conclusions

Make a distinction

What is the premise

What ideas apply, do not
 apply

Implicit in the statement is
 the idea of

What statement is relevant,
 extraneous to, related to,
 not applicable

What does the author believe,
 assume

State the point of view of

What ideas justify the
 conclusion that

The least essential statements are

What's the theme, main idea,
 subordinate idea

What is the function of	What literary form is used
What's fact, opinion	What persuasive technique
What inconsistencies, fallacies are there	What is the relationship between

V. Synthesis (combining elements into a pattern not clearly there before)

Write (according to the following limitations)	Solve the following
	Plan
Create	Design
Tell	Make up
Make	Compose
Do	Formulate a theory
Dance	How else would you
Choose	State a rule
How would you test	Develop
Propose an alternative	

VI. Evaluation (according to some set of criteria, and state reasons for your evaluations)

Appraise	What fallacies, consistencies, inconsistencies appear
Judge	Which is more important, moral,
Criticize	better, logical, valid,
Defend	appropriate, inappropriate
Compare	Find the errors

Based on *Bloom's Taxonomy, Developed and Expanded* by John Maynard, Pomona, CA. The document is copyrighted by the TESA Program, Los Angeles County Office of Education, Phone: 1-800-566-6651.

REFLECTION

> How can I integrate Strategy 1: Brainstorming/Discussion into my lesson plans so that my students' brains are engaged?

Standard/Objective:_____

_____.

Activity:_____

_____.

Standard/Objective:_____

_____.

Activity:_____

_____.

Standard/Objective:_____

_____.

Activity:_____

_____.

Standard/Objective:_____

_____.

Activity:_____

_____.

Standard/Objective:_____

_____.

Activity:_____

_____.

Standard/Objective:_____

_____.

Activity:_____

_____.

Strategy 2

Drawing and Artwork

WHAT: DEFINING THE STRATEGY

Artists, interior designers, and architects are all professionals who have the amazing ability to perceive and transform the visual–spatial world around them. This ability serves them well in the real world but not always in traditional school settings.

For almost three decades, I have observed from the rear of classrooms as teachers imparted important content in the front. I have often watched students (perhaps future professional artists or architects) engaged in off-task behavior, intently drawing wonderfully artistic pictures of cars, creatures, superheroes, and other subjects of greater interest than the math or science being taught.

What do you suppose would happen if that artistic ability, that spatial intelligence, were put to instructional use? How many vocabulary words could students actually acquire if they could illustrate the definitions rather than merely looking them up in the dictionary or glossary and writing down the first definition they encounter? Brain and learning style theories support the idea that drawing strengthens memory, not only for vocabulary, but also for everything else.

HOW: SAMPLE CLASSROOM ACTIVITIES

- Level/Subject Area: Elementary/Middle/High (Cross-curricular)

Standard/Objective:	Increase vocabulary meaning.
Activity:	Students are given an opportunity to create a personal "pictionary" by illustrating assigned vocabulary words. Each page of the pictionary consists of an assigned word written

9

WHY: RESEARCH RATIONALE

Thinking in art precedes improvements in thinking in other curricular areas. (Dewey, 1934)

Students who have spatial intelligence are *picture smart* with the ability to graphically represent visual or spatial ideas. (Armstrong, 1994)

A seven-month study of 96 first graders resulted in significantly higher reading and math test scores for those in arts-enriched classes as opposed to those who experienced the standard curriculum. (Gardiner, 1996)

A strategy known as *visualizing vocabulary* enables students who are stronger in spatial rather than in verbal linguistic intelligence to find or draw pictures that illustrate the definitions of words. (Silver, Strong, & Commander, 1998)

Drawing figures helped improve critical thinking and verbal skills in learning-disabled children. (Jing, Yuan, & Liu, 1999)

Drawing is a tool that can be used to facilitate students' use of visualization. (Ogle, 2000)

Drawing is a strategy that makes use of Gardner's spatial intelligence or the capacity to perceive, create, and re-create pictures and images. (Silver, Strong, & Perini, 2000)

Different types of art activate different areas of the brain, including the thalamus and the amygdala. (Jensen, 2001)

Based on 1999 and 2000 test results, students who took studio art, art appreciation, and art design scored 47 points higher on the mathematics and 31 points higher on the verbal portion of college entrance exams than did those students who were not enrolled in visual arts classes. (College Board, 2000)

Students enrolled in visual arts programs, including painting classes and sculpture, consistently report gains in self-discipline, work ethic, and teamwork. (Jensen, 2001)

in color, a drawing that depicts the meaning of the word, and an original sentence using the word in the appropriate context.

- Level/Subject Area: Elementary/Middle/High (English/Language Arts)

  Standard/Objective: Identify an implicit main idea in a story or passage.

Activity: Students design a book jacket or cover that depicts their understanding of the major idea of a book or story previously read.

• Level/Subject Area: Elementary/Middle/High (Cross-curricular)

Standard/Objective: Recall the major details of a unit of study.

Activity: Students design a poster that illustrates the major details of a specific unit concept or unit of study, for example, five characteristics of the planet Mars or the three major land forms in the state of Georgia.

• Level/Subject Area: Elementary/Middle/High (Cross-curricular)

Standard/Objective: Review content previously taught.

Activity: Students draw a picture that depicts their understanding of content covered during a previous class session.

• Level/Subject Area: Elementary/Middle/High (Mathematics)

Standard/Objective: Determine the necessary operation in a word problem.

Activity: Students read a word problem and then draw a series of pictures that illustrate their understanding of what is actually happening in the problem. They then use the pictures to assist them in writing the numerical symbols for the word problem.

• Level/Subject Area: Elementary/Middle/High (Science)

Standard/Objective: Explain the function of the human body.

Activity: Students draw and label a particular part or process of the human body, for example, heart, lungs, digestive process.

- Level/Subject Area: Elementary/Middle/High (Cross-curricular)

Standard/Objective:	Recall information regarding a person or group of people.
Activity:	Students draw a stick person symbol. They attach notes about a person or group of people in eight areas to the appropriate spot on the stick figure: ideas to the brain, hopes or vision to the eyes, words to the mouth, actions to the hands, feelings to the heart, movement to the feet, weaknesses to the Achilles tendon, and strengths to the arm muscle (Sousa, 2001).

REFLECTION

> How can I integrate Strategy 2: Drawing/Artwork into my lesson plans so that my students' brains are engaged?

Standard/Objective:_____

_____.

Activity:_____

_____.

Standard/Objective:_____

_____.

Activity:_____

_____.

Standard/Objective:_____

_____.

Activity:_____

_____.

Standard/Objective:_____

_____.

Activity:_____

_____.

Standard/Objective:_____

_____.

Activity:_____

_____.

Standard/Objective:_____

_____.

Activity:_____

_____.

Strategy 3

Field Trips

WHAT: DEFINING THE STRATEGY

Many will recall a commercial for Bell South in which a cute, rambunctious, and bored little boy jumps up in the middle of class and yells *"FIELD TRIP!"* The entire class then quickly beats a path out the door.

Even if you've never seen the commercial, you will remember, no doubt, a time when you got on the little yellow school bus and journeyed to a distant location to accomplish a curricular objective. I still remember milking Rosebud, the cow, at the Mathis Dairy or listening, with my class, to the melodic sounds of the Atlanta Symphony Orchestra.

Field trips provide students with real-world experiences that make the subsequent learning more understandable and memorable. In this new millennium, an additional option exists—to plan virtual field trips that carry students to places that would otherwise be inaccessible or cost prohibitive.

HOW: SAMPLE CLASSROOM ACTIVITIES

- Level/Subject: Elementary/Middle (Mathematics)

    Standard/Objective: Calculate percentages.

    Activity: Students find coupons in the
    newspaper reflecting an amount of
    savings on five of their favorite foods.
    As a homework assignment, students
    actually go to the grocery store and
    purchase the items selected. They
    then calculate what percentage of the
    total cost they saved by using the
    coupons.

WHY: RESEARCH RATIONALE

Field trips have existed for thousands of years since some of the greatest teachers, Aristotle and Socrates, used them as instructional tools. (Krepel & Duvall, 1981)

Results of numerous research studies overwhelmingly concluded that experience outside the classroom consistently provides significant gains in both cognitive and affective achievement for all students, for all grade levels, and particularly for students categorized as at-risk. (Rudman, 1994)

The field trip must be linked to a curricular objective. (Millan, 1995)

Students experience a greater benefit when the educational experience is closer to reality. (Millan, 1995)

The Internet provides learning opportunities that were once unavailable to students, and it allows teachers easy access to curricular materials. (Mandel, 1998)

Teacher-constructed "cyber-trips" must involve a number of different Web sites that will provide a variety of experiences for students. (Mandel, 1998)

Students must see for themselves the connection between what the curriculum is teaching and their own experiences in order to link new learning to prior knowledge. (Lieberman & Miller, 2000)

Adolescents' schoolwork must carry them into the "dynamic life of their environments." (Brooks, 2002, p. 72)

- Level/Subject: Elementary/Middle/High (Cross-curricular)

  Standard/Objective: Reinforce curricular objectives via field trips.

  Activity: Select a site to visit that will reinforce a curricular objective. Consider visiting the site prior to unit instruction so that students have real-world images to help them clarify concepts.

- Level/Subject: Elementary/Middle (Science)

  Standard/Objective: Recall information regarding the solar system.

  Activity: Prior to a unit of study on the solar system, students visit a planetarium

where they actually see replicas of
what they will be studying
including the planets, constellations,
and so on.

- Level/Subject: Elementary/Middle/High (Cross-curricular)

Standard/Objective:	Reinforce curricular objectives via field trips.
Activity:	Contact the *Field Trip Factory* via its e-mail address to create and arrange a field trip that reinforces a curricular objective and enables students to learn valuable life skills that will help them live healthier lives: info@FieldTripFactory.com

- Level/Subject: Elementary/Middle/High (Cross-curricular)

Standard/Objective:	Design a virtual field trip around a curricular objective.
Activity:	Locate a search engine such as Infoseek or Lycos and type in a specific key term for the unit of study. The more specific the term can be, the more focused the search. The search engine Metacrawler searches all the other search engines to supply teachers with the top 10 links for virtual field trips.

- Level/Subject: Elementary/Middle/High (Cross-curricular)

Standard/Objective:	Design a virtual field trip around a curricular objective.
Activity:	Connect to the Internet and type the words *field trip*. You will discover many sites that will help you plan a virtual field trip. Examples of the sites include www.field-guides.com, www.tramline.com, antwrp.gsfc. nasa.gov, and www.mcps.k12.md.us

- Level/Subject: Elementary/Middle/High (Mathematics)

Standard/Objective:	Design and solve real-world problems in the school environment.
Activity:	Students walk around their community and create real-world mathematics problems based on what they discover. The teacher then submits the problems, along with any accompanying photographs, recordings, videos, and so on, to the National Math Trails Web site. The problems are posted by grade level for students throughout the country to solve.

REFLECTION

> How can I integrate Strategy 3: Field Trips into my lesson plans so that my students' brains are engaged?

Standard/Objective:_____

_____.

Activity:_____

_____.

Standard/Objective:_____

_____.

Activity:_____

_____.

Standard/Objective:_____

_____.

Activity:_____

_____.

Standard/Objective:_____

_____.

Activity:_____

_____.

Standard/Objective:_____

_____.

Activity:_____

_____.

Standard/Objective:_____

_____.

Activity:_____

_____.

Standard/Objective:_____

_____.

Activity:_____

_____.

Strategy 4

Games

WHAT: DEFINING THE STRATEGY

Mrs. Edwards, a fourth grade teacher at Chapel Hill Elementary School, was having a difficult time getting students to pass her social studies tests. At the time she spoke with me, the highest score that any student was able to achieve was 74. She stated that students simply were not reviewing the information and studying at home for the tests.

I recommended that before she tested for the next chapter, she use a game to review the information. She did exactly that and with very favorable results. On the next test, the *lowest* score that any student made was a 76 and the class average was an 88.

Mrs. Edwards had selected key points in the chapter and turned them into answers for a *Jeopardy!* board. Students competed against one another to come up with the questions that accompanied the designated answers. I was actually invited to the classroom to watch the game in progress. It didn't even seem to be the same classroom. Students were motivated and actively engaged in supplying as many questions as quickly as possible for the answers provided. What a difference! All because of a little motivational thing called a game.

HOW: SAMPLE CLASSROOM ACTIVITIES

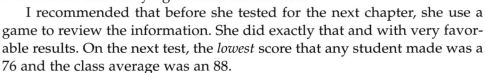

- Level/Subject Area: Elementary/Middle/High (Cross-curricular)

    Standard/Objective: Review content previously taught.

    Activity: Students work in cooperative
                               groups to construct an original
                               game board according to the
                               following guidelines: they must

WHY: RESEARCH RATIONALE

Even adults are activating the brain when they participate in *Jeopardy!* shows. (Jensen, 1995)

Allowing learners to redesign any game that they already know, such as *Wheel of Fortune, Simon Sez, Concentration,* or *Ball Toss,* provides the brain connections necessary for a better understanding of the alternative content. (Jensen, 1995)

Games use the most basic level of active processing, creative rehearsal. (Caine & Caine, 1997)

Human play fulfills the body's need to express emotions, to bond with others socially, and to explore new learning with challenge, feedback, and success. (Beyers, 1998)

The mechanisms involved when students are playing a game are just as cognitive as when students are doing math seatwork. (Bjorkland & Brown, 1998)

Play is the brain's link from the inner world to reality and the foundation of creativity. (Jensen, 2001)

Play speeds up the brain's maturation process since it involves the built-in processes of challenge, novelty, feedback, coherence, and time. (Jensen, 2001)

The effectiveness of a game is enhanced when students actually help to design or construct it. (Wolfe, 2001)

provide 30 spaces including a *begin* and an *end* space, two *move ahead* spaces, and two *go back* spaces. Students make game question cards appropriate to whatever content needs to be reviewed. They also provide an accompanying answer key. Each group of students uses another group's game board and questions. Each group reviews content by rolling a number generator (die), moving the rolled number of spaces, selecting a card, and answering the designated question. The first student in each group to get to the end of the game board wins.

- Level/Subject Area: Elementary/Middle/High (Cross-curricular)

Standard/Objective:	Recall information previously read or taught.
Activity:	Students construct a *Jeopardy!* game by selecting key points in a designated chapter that can serve as answers. Answers are placed on a class game board in categories of 100, 200, 300, 400, and 500 points. The easiest answers are worth 100 and the most difficult, 500. Students form teams and take turns providing the questions for the designated answers. The game proceeds according to the rules for playing the television show *Jeopardy!*

- Level/Subject Area: Elementary/Middle/High (Cross-curricular)

Standard/Objective:	Expand vocabulary development.
Activity:	Students make 15 matched pairs of vocabulary words and their definitions. They write each word on one index card and the accompanying definition on another. They then spread the word and definition cards out face-down in random order. Students work in pairs to match the word to its appropriate definition. One match entitles the student to another try. The student with the most matches at the end of the game wins.

- Level/Subject Area: Elementary/Middle/High (Cross-curricular)

Standard/Objective:	Spells words correctly.
Activity:	Students play *Wheel of Fortune* with partners. Each partner selects a vocabulary or spelling word from a list provided by the teacher and has the partner guess the word by guessing one letter at a time. Partner 1 fills in each correct letter as it is guessed. Then Partner 2 has a turn. The partner to correctly guess a word in the shortest amount of time is the winner.

- Level/Subject Area: Elementary/Middle/High (Cross-curricular)

Standard/Objective:	Involve all students in answering questions.
Activity:	When a question is asked, toss a Nerf or other soft ball to the student who is to respond. The student gets one point for catching the ball and two points for answering the question correctly. This student can then randomly pick the student who will answer the next question and toss the ball to that student.

- Level/Subject Area: Elementary/Middle/High (Cross-curricular)

Standard/Objective:	Expand vocabulary development.
Activity:	Students compete in pairs and take turns being the first to get their partners to guess a designated word by providing them with a one-word synonym or definition for the vocabulary word. The point value begins at 10 and decreases by one each time the word is not guessed. This game is patterned after the game *Password*.

- Level/Subject Area: Elementary/Middle/High (Cross-curricular)

Standard/Objective:	Recall information from a unit of study.
Activity:	Following a unit of study and prior to the test, students work in heterogeneous groups to write ten questions at varying levels of difficulty with four possible answer choices. Each question is assigned a monetary level of difficulty in $100 increments ranging from $100 to $1,000. They also write three more difficult questions worth $5,000, $25,000, and $100,000, respectively. Student groups compete to earn money for their team by answering another team's questions. This game is adapted from the game show *Who Wants to Be a Millionaire?*

- Level/Subject Area: Elementary/Middle/High (Cross-curricular)

Standard/Objective:	Recall famous literary or historical figures.
Activity:	Students play the *Who Am I?* game by providing written clues regarding a famous literary or historical figure being studied. Students take turns reading their clues aloud as class members try to guess the identity of the figure. Students earn a point for every time the class fails to guess the person described.

- Level/Subject Area: Elementary/Middle/High (Cross-curricular)

Standard/Objective:	Expand vocabulary development.
Activity:	Provide students with a bingo card containing 25 blank spaces. Students write vocabulary words randomly in any space on their card. Have students take turns randomly pulling from a bag and reading the definitions of the designated words. Students cover each word as the appropriate definition is read. The first student to cover five words in a row, horizontally, vertically, or diagonally, wins.

REFLECTION

How can I integrate Strategy 4: Games into my lesson plans so that my students' brains are engaged?

Standard/Objective:_____
_____.

Activity:_____
_____.

Standard/Objective:_____
_____.

Activity:_____
_____.

Standard/Objective:_____
_____.

Activity:_____
_____.

Standard/Objective:_____
_____.

Activity:_____
_____.

Standard/Objective:_____
_____.

Activity:_____
_____.

Standard/Objective:_____
_____.

Activity:_____
_____.

Graphic Organizers, Semantic Maps, and Word Webs

WHAT: DEFINING THE STRATEGY

Some students at Stone Mountain Middle School were having a difficult time following the lectures of their content-area teachers. I was asked to conduct an inservice that provided strategies for making difficult or highly technical information easier to understand. Since I had a limited amount of time that afternoon, I decided to concentrate on the one strategy I thought would make the most difference. You guessed it—the use of graphic organizers or semantic maps. I taught teachers to draw mind maps on the board as they lectured, ones that would show relationships between the major concepts being taught. I later learned that student grades began to improve almost immediately. I assume I was right in my selection of this time-tested technique.

Graphic organizers are visual representations of linear ideas and benefit both left and right hemispheres of the brain. They assist us in making sense of information and enable us to search for patterns. Graphic organizers, also known as word webs or semantic, mind, and concept maps, can be used to plan lessons or present information to students. Once familiar with the technique, students should be able to construct their own graphic organizers, reflecting their understanding of the concepts taught.

WHY: RESEARCH RATIONALE

Ten years of research indicate that graphic organizers constructed before reading facilitate comprehension for elementary students while graphic organizers constructed after reading result in improved vocabulary and comprehension scores for secondary students. (Dunston, 1992)

Mind mapping engages all the brain's functions and captures the total picture. (Buzan & Buzan, 1994)

Concept mapping integrates the visual and the verbal which enhances understanding of concepts whether they are verbal, or nonverbal, concrete or abstract. (Sousa, 1995)

Graphic organizers meet the needs of students with a variety of learning styles and ability levels since they contain both visual and verbal information. (Bromley, Irwin-De Vitis, & Modlo, 1995)

After examining 135 studies, Luiten concluded that forms of advanced organizers gave learners ways to conceptualize ideas, structure their thinking, better comprehend what they know and solidify the learning as theirs. (Jensen, 1996)

Graphic organizers such as the concept map, the web, and the Venn diagram make thinking visible to the students. (Fogarty, 1997)

Graphic organizers provide connections among bits of information, make information easier to remember, and allow students to break information into meaningful chunks. (Parry & Gregory, 1998)

Graphic organizers help students make content connections that show how the information is related. (Kagan, 1998)

Graphic organizers, probably the most widely used bridge to visualization, provide an alternative to the traditional outlining and notetaking of ideas. (Ogle, 2000)

Using systematic visual or semantic graphs regarding the content of a social studies or science passage facilitates memory and content area achievement. (Report of the National Reading Panel, 2000)

HOW: SAMPLE CLASSROOM ACTIVITIES

- Level/Subject Area: Elementary/Middle/High (Cross-curricular)

Standard/Objective:	Access prior knowledge and summarize content learned.
Activity:	Students complete the following K-N-L graphic organizer by brainstorming (1) what they already *Know* about a new concept or unit

of study, (2) what they will *Need* to know, and, following the completion of the unit, (3) what they *Learned*.

The K-N-L Strategy		
Topic:_____		
What I Know	What I Need to Know	What I Learned

- Level/Subject Area: Elementary/Middle/High (Cross-curricular)

    Standard/Objective: Increase vocabulary meaning.

    Activity: As a new vocabulary word is introduced, students complete the word web below by brainstorming additional synonyms for the new word. Students may keep their word webs in a notebook for review and add synonyms throughout the year. They should be encouraged to add these words to their speaking and writing vocabularies as well.

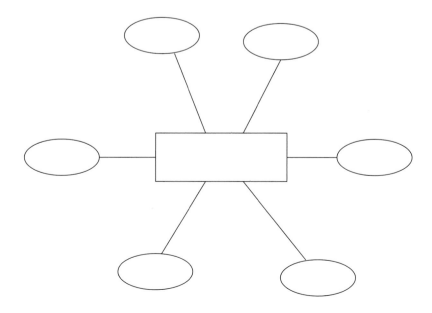

- Level/Subject Area: Elementary/Middle/High (Cross-curricular)

  Standard/Objective: Comprehend story plot.

  Activity: Following the reading of a story, students complete the following story frame to demonstrate their understanding of story plot.

Story Map

Title: _____

Setting: [   ]

Characters:_____   _____
            _____   _____
            _____   _____

                        [   ]

Problem:
Event 1   _____
Event 2   _____
Event 3   _____
Event 4   _____

    Solution   [   ]

- Level/Subject Area: Elementary/Middle/High (Cross-curricular)

  Standard/Objective: Identify the main idea and details in narrative or content-area texts.

  Activity: Students complete the following graphic organizer to demonstrate their understanding that supporting details in a passage should add up to the main idea.

Main Idea/Details

Details

+

Main Idea

- Level/Subject Area: Elementary/Middle/High (Cross-curricular)

Standard/Objective:	Identify cause–effect relationships in narrative and content-area texts.
Activity:	Students complete the following graphic organizer to demonstrate their understanding that every action has an effect.

Cause/Effect

So

	→	

	→	

	→	

	→	

- Level/Subject Area: Elementary/Middle/High (Cross-curricular)

Standard/Objective: Identify character traits in narrative and content-area texts.

Activity: Students complete the following graphic organizer to demonstrate their understanding of a character's traits and provide evidence to support the traits.

Character Traits

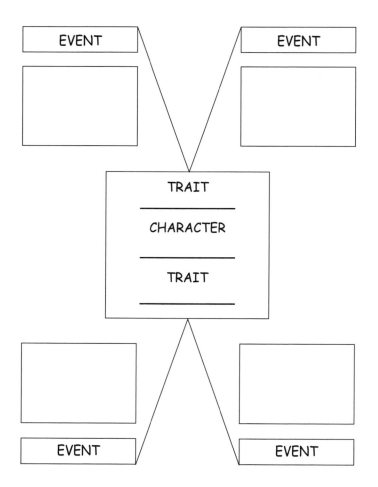

- Level/Subject Area: Elementary/Middle/High (Cross-curricular)

Standard/Objective:	Identify sequence of events in narrative and content-area texts.
Activity:	Students complete the following graphic organizer to demonstrate their understanding of sequence of events.

SEQUENCE

```
┌─────────────────────────────┐
│                             │
└─────────────────────────────┘

┌─────────────────────────────────┐
│                                 │
└─────────────────────────────────┘
               ▼
┌─────────────────────────────────┐
│                                 │
└─────────────────────────────────┘
               ▼
┌─────────────────────────────────┐
│                                 │
└─────────────────────────────────┘
               ▼
┌─────────────────────────────────┐
│                                 │
└─────────────────────────────────┘
               ▼
┌─────────────────────────────────┐
│                                 │
└─────────────────────────────────┘
```

- Level/Subject Area: Elementary/Middle/High (Cross-curricular)

Standard/Objective:	Compare and contrast two characters or events in narrative and content-area texts.
Activity:	Students complete the following Venn diagram to demonstrate their understanding of comparing and contrasting two concepts.

COMPARE/CONTRAST

Different   Alike   Different

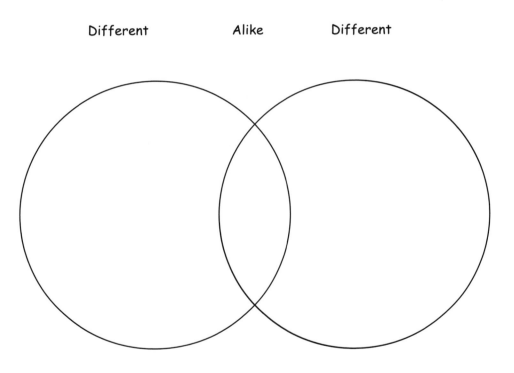

- Level/Subject Area: Elementary/Middle/High (Cross-curricular)

  Standard/Objective: Comprehend the relationships between concepts presented in a lecture or unit of study.

  Activity: While lecturing or as students read a unit of study, complete a semantic, concept, or mind map to show how the major concepts are related to one another. (See the example below.) Have students copy the semantic map in their notes. Encourage them to make mind maps of their own as they master this type of graphic organizer.

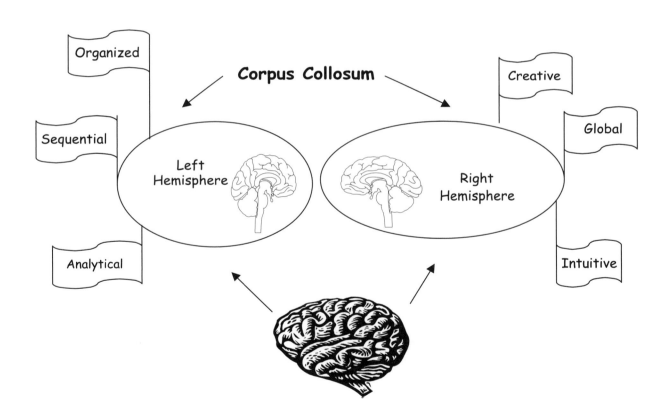

REFLECTION

> How can I integrate Strategy 5: Graphic Organizers/Semantic Maps/Word Webs into my lesson plans so that my students' brains are engaged?

Standard/Objective:_____

_____.

Activity:_____

_____.

Standard/Objective:_____

_____.

Activity:_____

_____.

Standard/Objective:_____

_____.

Activity:_____

_____.

Standard/Objective:_____

_____.

Activity:_____

_____.

Standard/Objective:_____

_____.

Activity:_____

_____.

Standard/Objective:_____

_____.

Activity:_____

_____.

Strategy 6

Humor

WHAT: DEFINING THE STRATEGY

Most people enjoy a good joke. However, research (Jensen, 1995; Sousa, 2001; Sylwester, 1997) shows that jokes, riddles, celebrations, and other forms of positive interaction not only create a positive learning environment but may also facilitate the learning itself. Starting a lesson with a joke or humorous story is a good way to get the learner's attention. As the lesson proceeds, David Sousa (2001) suggests that students can actually benefit from taking their work seriously and themselves lightly.

The use of humor in the classroom is not to be confused with sarcasm, which has the exact opposite effect on the brains of students. The literal definition of sarcasm is *a tearing of the flesh,* aptly named since remarks directed to students that demean, tease, or deride can, at minimum, hinder or incapacitate higher level thinking (Jensen, 1995).

In addition to the activities listed below, refer to Chapter 4, Games, for additional strategies that result in a positive classroom environment and lots of laughter.

HOW: SAMPLE CLASSROOM ACTIVITIES

- Level/Subject Area: Elementary/Middle/High (Cross-curricular)

Standard/Objective:	Involve all students in a lesson.
Activity:	There are humorous ways to randomly involve students in lessons. For students who are working in cooperative groups, when it is time to select a spokesperson for the group, students point into the air and then, on the count of three, point to the

WHY: RESEARCH RATIONALE

Researchers at Stanford University have discovered that laughter causes biochemical changes in the body, such as an increase in white blood cell activity and changes in the chemical balance of the blood, resulting in an increase in the body's production of neurotransmitters necessary for alertness and memory. (Jensen, 1995)

A good laugh has the ability to lower brain and body stress resulting in a better learner. (Jensen, 1995)

Positive feedback may be the one most dynamic influence on the brain's chemistry and is essential for the development of a positive self-concept and healthy self-esteem. (Sylwester, 1997)

There is a direct correlation between a positive experience, improved memory, and actual performance. (Pert, 1997)

Class material taught in the form of a joke was recalled better both immediately and later than material taught in text sentences. (Derks, Gardner, & Agarwal, 1998)

Laughter increases the number of type T leukocytes (T cells) in the blood, cells that strengthen the immune system and combat infection and damage to the body. (Cardoso, 2000)

Laughter and humor maintain students' attention, reduce mental and physical tension, relieve stress, and make the school day shorter. (Burgess, 2000)

Laughter causes the release of endorphins in the bloodstream, neurotransmitters that give the body a feeling of wellness and euphoria. (Sousa, 2001)

When students laugh together, they bond together and create a community spirit conducive to learning. (Sousa, 2001)

Energizing cheers incorporate both aural and kinesthetic actions that help energize the body by sending more oxygen and glucose to the brain. (Gregory & Chapman, 2002)

person in the group they want to be spokesperson. The student with the most fingers pointing at him or her becomes the spokesperson.

Adaptation: Select students according to the following additional categories:
1. Students wearing red (or any other color)
2. Students wearing contacts or glasses

3. Students wearing jewelry such as rings or earrings
4. Students who have brothers, sisters, or pets
5. Students who live closest to or farthest from school

Students may also make up additional humorous categories for selecting peers to fulfill other cooperative group roles (i.e., presenter, recorder, materials handler, timekeeper).

- Level/Subject Area: Elementary/Middle/High (Cross-curricular)

    Standard/Objective: Comprehend concepts taught.

    Activity: Locate or create and incorporate cartoons, riddles, and jokes which reinforce a concept to be taught into the delivery of instruction.

- Level/Subject Area: Elementary/Middle/High (Cross-curricular)

    Standard/Objective: Comprehend concepts taught.

    Activity: Students design cartoons or humorous stories that demonstrate their understanding of a concept taught.

Source: National Council of Teachers of Mathematics, 1970.

- Level/Subject Area: Elementary/Middle/High (Cross-curricular)

    Standard/Objective: Comprehend concepts taught.

    Activity: Students work individually or in cooperative groups to design riddles that demonstrate their understanding of a concept taught. Students then work to solve one another's riddles. For example: Question: What is one flower that does not grow in the ground? Answer: The Mayflower.

- Level/Subject Area: Elementary/Middle/High (Cross-curricular)

Standard/Objective:	Comprehend concepts taught.
Activity:	Students work individually or in cooperative groups to design jokes that demonstrate their understanding of a concept taught.

- Level/Subject Area: Elementary/Middle/High (Cross-curricular)

Standard/Objective:	Provide positive feedback for appropriate responses. Celebrate learning.
Activity:	Students celebrate appropriate answers given by peers. These might include, but are not limited to, the following: applause, thumbs-up, high-fives, and original cheers.

- Level/Subject Area: Elementary/Middle/High (Cross-curricular)

Standard/Objective:	Provide positive feedback for appropriate responses. Celebrate learning.
Activity:	Provide positive feedback for correct student responses in humorous ways, such as providing applause via a hand clapper, blowing bubbles, blowing a paper horn, or high-fiving the student.

- Level/Subject Area: Elementary/Middle/High (Cross-curricular)

Standard/Objective:	Create an environment conducive to optimal learning.
Activity:	Place humorous signs around the room. For example: "Knowledge given away here, free. Bring your own container" (Burgess, 2000, p. 20).

REFLECTION

> How can I integrate Strategy 6: Humor into my lesson plans so that my students' brains are engaged?

Standard/Objective:_____

_____.

Activity:_____

_____.

Standard/Objective:_____

_____.

Activity:_____

_____.

Standard/Objective:_____

_____.

Activity:_____

_____.

Standard/Objective:_____

_____.

Activity:_____

_____.

Standard/Objective:_____

_____.

Activity:_____

_____.

Standard/Objective:_____

_____.

Activity:_____

_____.

Manipulatives, Experiments, Labs, and Models

WHAT: DEFINING THE STRATEGY

My daughter, Jennifer, took chemistry when she was in 10th grade. As I followed her progress during the semester, I noticed the 100% average that she achieved on her laboratory assignments. However, she was not faring as well on the teacher-made objective tests. Paper and pencil tests have never been her strong suit. I did not become concerned until I realized that Jennifer's lab grades only contributed to 10% of her overall semester average. The more I thought about what actual chemists do, such as lab work, the more I realized that students are often penalized in school for being proficient at skills that would serve them well in the real world. After all, when is the last time a chemist walked into the lab, sat down, and took a paper and pencil test?

My son, Christopher, has difficulty paying attention in class when the teacher lectures for most of the period. However, this is the same teenager who can spend hours in his room constructing a moving car out of K'nex blocks or who excels in a summer hands-on science camp sponsored by the Georgia Institute of Technology.

Both of these students, and many others like them, probably possess what Howard Gardner calls bodily-kinesthetic intelligence. This type of intelligence includes not only expertise in physical skills, but specific haptic or tactile capabilities as well. These students usually excel with hands-on strategies such as using manipulatives, conducting experiments, and constructing models.

WHY: RESEARCH RATIONALE

Those who have expertise in bodily-kinesthetic intelligence can easily use their hands to either produce or change things in the real world (e.g., a sculptor, mechanic, or surgeon). (Armstrong, 1994)

There should be materials in the classroom that provide opportunities for students to manipulate, build, or encounter other hands-on experiences. (Armstrong, 1994)

Those with bodily-kinesthetic intelligence possess a sensitivity to touch, movement, the physical self, and athleticism. (Silver et al., 2000)

Each body movement stimulates an area of the brain's cortex at slightly different times similar to a well-timed explosion in the head. (Calvin, 1996)

The best teaching techniques for fostering intelligence unite (instead of separate) mind and body. (Wilson, 1999)

Kinesthetic arts enhance the development of critical emotional, immune, and perceptual-motor neurobiological systems. (Jensen, 2001)

Implicit learning, which includes body and hands-on learning, is lasting, independent of age, easy to acquire, cross-cultural, and independent of measures of intelligence. (Jensen, 2001)

Kinesthetic learners are at their best when engaged in physical movement or when completing meaningful real-life learning activities. (Gregory & Chapman, 2002)

Brain activity and the use of the hands are so interrelated and complicated that there is not one brain theory that explains it. (Jensen, 2001)

Kinesthetic actions energize students by allowing increased oxygen and glucose to get to the brain. (Gregory & Chapman, 2002)

HOW: SAMPLE CLASSROOM ACTIVITIES

- Level/Subject Area: Elementary/Middle/High (Mathematics)

  Standard/Objective: Apply a mathematics concept.

  Activity: Students use tiles, blocks, or Cuisenaire rods during mathematics instruction to display their understanding of a particular concept.

- Level/Subject Area: Elementary/Middle/High (Science)

   Standard/Objective: Demonstrate understanding of a scientific concept.

   Activity: Students follow directions to complete an experiment or lab to demonstrate their understanding of a concept previously taught.

- Level/Subject Area: Elementary (Cross-curricular)

   Standard/Objective: Spell words correctly.

   Activity: Students practice spelling or content-area vocabulary words in a number of haptic or tactile ways including the following: writing them in the air, writing them in shaving cream spread on the desk, forming them with clay or other pliable materials, or using magnetic alphabet letters to build the words.

- Level/Subject Area: Elementary/Middle/High (Cross-curricular)

   Standard/Objective: Demonstrate understanding of a concept previously taught.

   Activity: Students construct models which show their understanding of a concept previously taught. For example, students construct a model of the solar system that shows the planets in order from the sun to Pluto, or they build adobe huts that show how Native Americans once lived.

- Level/Subject Area: Elementary (Mathematics)

   Standard/Objective: Comprehend the concept of fractions.

   Activity: Students are given pieces of construction paper and asked to place the pieces in the shape of a pizza. Some students have two pieces, some four pieces, and some have eight pieces, all which form whole pizzas. Students assemble the pieces and then compare the sizes of their pieces with other classmates. They are asked to make assumptions regarding the sizes of the pieces, becoming familiar with terms such as halves, fourths, and eighths.

- Level/Subject Area: Elementary/Middle/High (Cross-curricular)

Standard/Objective:	Involve all students in the lesson.
Activity:	Students use their hands to show agreement or disagreement with an answer or levels of understanding for an answer by doing one of the following:

Thumbs up: agree
Thumbs down: don't agree
Five fingers: completely
   understand
One finger: don't understand
Pat head: understand
Scratch head: don't understand.

REFLECTION

> How can I integrate Strategy 7: Manipulatives/Experiments/Labs/Models into my lesson plans so that my students' brains are engaged?

Standard/Objective:_____

_____.

Activity:_____

_____.

Standard/Objective:_____

_____.

Activity:_____

_____.

Standard/Objective:_____

_____.

Activity:_____

_____.

Standard/Objective:_____

_____.

Activity:_____

_____.

Standard/Objective:_____

_____.

Activity:_____

_____.

Standard/Objective:_____

_____.

Activity:_____

_____.

Strategy 8

Metaphors, Analogies, and Similes

WHAT: DEFINING THE STRATEGY

The fog comes in on little cat feet.
Shakespeare : Hamlet :: Charles Dickens : A Christmas Carol
My love is like a red, red rose.

What possible relationship could Carl Sandburg think existed between the fog and a cat's feet? How are Shakespeare and *Hamlet* related and how does that compare to the correlation between Charles Dickens and *A Christmas Carol*? How can love be like a red rose? Good writers know about the strategy of metaphor, analogy, and simile and use it consistently to enhance their craft.

Strategy 8 is probably the most powerful of the 20 strategies. Students can understand many new and complicated concepts when those concepts are compared to dissimilar ones that the student already knows and understands.

As a meaning maker, the brain is constantly searching for connections and patterns. People who think metaphorically can see connections where others cannot. Therefore, successful teachers should be constantly assisting students in making connections and seeing patterns between the new and the known.

WHY: RESEARCH RATIONALE

Most of our normal system of concepts is metaphorically structured; in other words, most concepts are understood only as they relate to other concepts. (Lakoff & Johnson, 1980)

Metaphors must be used deliberately across the curriculum. (Gardner, 1983)

Students should make new learning fit into their personal world by capitalizing on the brain's ability to connect the new to the known. (Caine & Caine, 1994)

Making associations forms new connections between neurons and encodes new insights similar to a tree growing new branches. (Sousa, 1995)

Creating and analyzing metaphors to enhance meaning and higher-order thinking skills is a teaching strategy that involves left hemisphere skills. (Sousa, 1995)

Metaphors link abstract, difficult to understand concepts with personal experiences and promote a sense of creativity. (Whitin & Whitin, 1997)

Metaphors can make otherwise forgettable concepts memorable, placing them easily and quickly into the brain. (Deporter, Reardon, & Singer-Nourie, 1999)

Metaphor allows a concept to be viewed from a broader perspective, such as how it is applicable to other content areas, to the student's home environment, or to life as a whole. (Allen, 2002)

Comparing, contrasting, classifying, and using metaphors are all instructional strategies that increase student achievement. (Marzano, Pickering, & Pollack, 2001)

Metaphorical connections stretch the thinking of students and increase the likelihood that their understanding of a topic or concept will be broadened or retained in the future. (Gregory & Chapman, 2002)

HOW: SAMPLE CLASSROOM ACTIVITIES

- Level/Subject Area: Elementary/Middle/High (Cross-curricular)

  Standard/Objective: Comprehend new or difficult concepts.

  Activity: Whenever possible, introduce a new or difficult concept by comparing it to a concept the students already know and understand. For example, the French word *rouge* means red, which is similar to the makeup *rouge,* which women wear.

- **Level/Subject Area: Elementary (Language Arts)**

Standard/Objective:	Comprehend similes.
Activity:	Read aloud *I'm as Quick as a Cricket* by Audrey Wood. Students think of ways they are like animals and write a story using the following pattern: *I'm as _____as a _____.*

- **Level/Subject Area: Elementary (Reading/Language Arts)**

Standard/Objective:	Determine main idea and details.
Activity:	Compare the concept of main idea and details to a table with the following simile. Say, *A main idea and details are like a table with legs. A tabletop cannot stand alone and, therefore, is supported by legs. The tabletop is like a main idea in a story. The main idea also cannot stand alone and is supported by important details in the story.* Have the students draw a tabletop supported by four legs. Read a story and have students write the main idea on the tabletop and one supporting detail on each of the four legs.

- **Level/Subject Area: Elementary/Middle/High (Cross-curricular)**

Standard/Objective:	Comprehend the relationship between two concepts.
Activity:	Given the pattern a : b :: c : d (a is to b as c is to d), students create analogies that show how two sets of ideas or concepts are related. For example, Thomas Edison : light bulb :: Alexander Graham Bell : _____. Another student provides the missing word to complete each analogy.

- Level/Subject Area: Elementary/Middle/High (Cross-curricular)

Standard/Objective:	Compare and contrast two concepts or ideas.
Activity:	Students write metaphors that symbolize their understanding of two unrelated concepts. They explain the relationship between the two concepts to a partner. For example, Life is a journey. The brain is a computer.

- Level/Subject Area: Elementary/Middle/High (Cross-curricular)

Standard/Objective:	Recognize metaphors, analogies, and similes in print.
Activity:	Students pretend to be detectives and look for metaphors, analogies, and similes in narrative and expository texts. Post a list of the examples students find and periodically ask students to explain the relationships that exist between the two concepts.

- Level/Subject Area: Elementary/Middle/High (Cross-curricular)

Standard/Objective:	Use metaphors to compare two unrelated concepts.
Activity:	Students fill in the blanks. If ____were a _____, it would be ____ because _____. For example, If the brain were a piece of jewelry, it would be a chain because it has many links.

REFLECTION

> How can I integrate Strategy 8: Metaphors/Analogies/Similes into my lesson plans so that my students brains are engaged?

Standard/Objective:_____

_____.

Activity:_____

_____.

Standard/Objective:_____

_____.

Activity:_____

_____.

Standard/Objective:_____

_____.

Activity:_____

_____.

Standard/Objective:_____

_____.

Activity:_____

_____.

Standard/Objective:_____

_____.

Activity:_____

_____.

Standard/Objective:_____

_____.

Activity:_____

_____.

Strategy 9

Mnemonic Devices

WHAT: DEFINING THE STRATEGY

Good Boys Do Fine Always!
HOMES
When two vowels go walking, the first one does the talking.

Do these sound familiar? They should. These statements are samples of many of the mnemonic devices that our brains have heard repeatedly over the years. Due to the catchiness and repetitive nature of the words or sentences themselves, these statements have served to facilitate memory.

Mnemonic derives from the Greek term *mnema*, meaning memory, since this strategy serves as a very effective tool to aid memory. Mnemonics use the principle of association and include acronyms (i.e., Roy G. Biv for the colors of the rainbow—<u>r</u>ed, <u>o</u>range, <u>y</u>ellow, green, <u>b</u>lue, <u>i</u>ndigo, and <u>v</u>iolet) and acrostics. Acrostics are sentences in which the first letter in each word of the sentence actually represents the first letter in the concept to be memorized (i.e., <u>M</u>y <u>v</u>ery <u>e</u>ducated <u>m</u>other <u>j</u>ust <u>s</u>erved <u>u</u>s <u>n</u>ine <u>p</u>izzas actually represents the planets in order from the sun—<u>M</u>ercury, <u>V</u>enus, <u>E</u>arth, <u>M</u>ars, <u>J</u>upiter, <u>S</u>aturn, <u>U</u>ranus, <u>N</u>eptune, and <u>P</u>luto).

HOW: SAMPLE CLASSROOM ACTIVITIES

- Level/Subject Area: Elementary/Middle/High (Cross-curricular)

Standard/Objective:	Recall information previously taught.
Activity:	As concepts are taught, create mnemonic devices (rhymes, acronyms, or acrostics) to assist

---

WHY: RESEARCH RATIONALE

Factual information can be more easily applied when mnemonic devices are used to acquire the information. (Levin & Levin, 1990)

Special-needs first graders acquired letter-sound and letter-recognition skills more easily when picture mnemonics were integrated. (Fulk, Lohman, & Belfiore, 1997)

Reduction mnemonics takes a large amount of information and reduces it to a shorter form, which is easier for the brain to remember. (Pinkofsky & Reeves, 1998)

Mnemonic tools work because they provide the brain with powerful cues for recalling chunks of information. (Markowitz & Jensen, 1999)

According to research, people who use mnemonic devices learn two to three times more than those who learn normally. (Markowitz & Jensen, 1999)

Mnemonics increase the brain's ability to recall information and have been found to increase the ability of children who are crime victims to recall valuable information regarding the incident. (Aldridge, 1999)

Mnemonics help activate the creation of stronger neuro-links in the hippocampus, which are essential to short- and long-term memory. (Jensen, 2001)

The ancient Greeks considered the imagination and high-level thinking needed for the creation of mnemonics as essential to a classical education. (Wolfe, 2001)

Mnemonics create links or associations between new information the brain is receiving and information already stored in long-term memory. (Wolfe, 2001)

Mnemonics can be effectively used in various professions including education, medicine, law enforcement, and geriatric settings. (Jensen & Dabney, 2000)

---

students in remembering the most important concepts.

- Level/Subject Area: Elementary/Middle/High (Cross-curricular)

Standard/Objective:	Recall information previously taught.
Activity:	After being given numerous examples, students create slogans or phrases to help them understand and remember information that is

difficult to recall. For example,
*30 days hath September, April, June,
and November* . . . helps one to recall
the number of days in each month.

- Level/Subject Area: Elementary/Middle/High (Cross-curricular)

Standard/Objective:	Recall a series of items.
Activity:	After being given numerous examples, students create their own acrostic sentences to help them remember information that is difficult to recall. For example, <u>G</u>ood <u>B</u>oys <u>D</u>o <u>F</u>ine <u>A</u>lways represents the notes *GBDFA* on the bass clef of the scale.

- Level/Subject Area: Elementary/Middle/High (Cross-curricular)

Standard/Objective:	Recall information previously taught.
Activity:	After being given numerous examples, students create their own acronyms (words) to help them remember information that is difficult to recall. For example, *HOMES* represents the Great Lakes—<u>H</u>uron, <u>O</u>ntario, <u>M</u>ichigan, <u>E</u>rie, and <u>S</u>uperior.

- Level/Subject Area: Elementary/Middle/High (Cross-curricular)

Standard/Objective:	Recall a series of items.
Activity:	Students use *chunking* as a mnemonic device by linking items together with memorable associations. For example, students can remember the following list of numbers by making associations: 1492007200025 becomes Columbus sailed the ocean blue in 1492 with James Bond (007) at the turn of the century 2000 for a generation (25 years).

- Level/Subject Area: Elementary/Middle/High (Cross-curricular)

Standard/Objective:	Recognize mnemonic devices.

Activity: Students look for examples of
                             mnemonic devices in narrative and
                             expository texts. Post a list of
                             examples and review them
                             periodically to facilitate memory.

- Level/Subject Area: Elementary/Middle/High (Cross-curricular)

Standard/Objective: Recall a series of items in order.

Activity: Students use the *peg-word system*
                             and linking to remember items in
                             order. Students associate a rhyming
                             word with each number 1–10. For
                             example, 1 = bun, 2 = shoe, 3 = tree,
                             4 = door, 5 = hive, 6 = sticks,
                             7 = heaven, 8 = gate, 9 = sign,
                             10 = hen. They then link each item
                             on the list with the designated
                             rhyming word in the most absurd
                             visual possible. If the second item
                             on a grocery list is lettuce, the
                             student visualizes the lettuce in a
                             shoe (2) to remember that lettuce is
                             the second thing on the list.

REFLECTION

How can I integrate Strategy 9: Mnemonic Devices into my lesson plans so that my students' brains are engaged?

Standard/Objective:_____

_____.

Activity:_____

_____.

Standard/Objective:_____

_____.

Activity:_____

_____.

Standard/Objective:_____

_____.

Activity:_____

_____.

Standard/Objective:_____

_____.

Activity:_____

_____.

Standard/Objective:_____

_____.

Activity:_____

_____.

Standard/Objective:_____

_____.

Activity:_____

_____.

Strategy 10

Movement

WHAT: DEFINING THE STRATEGY

In most traditional classrooms, students sit for long periods of time in straight rows while important concepts are taught. Heaven forbid that any student should be *out of seat* during the process. Yet according to Eric Jensen (1995), more learning time is wasted by having students sit entirely too much. It is becoming abundantly clear (Wolfe, 2001) that movement for instructional reasons enhances memory for learning. According to Wolfe, adding movement provides extrasensory input to the brain and more than likely facilitates learning.

Whether students are holding words to form sentences; role-playing the chemical composition of solids, liquids, and gases; or revolving and rotating around the room to simulate the movement of the planets around the sun, movement is essential to retention of information. Note that movement and role play, Strategy 14, are practically synonymous. When students are acting out a concept, they are taking advantage of the power of movement at the very same time.

HOW: SAMPLE CLASSROOM ACTIVITIES

- Level/Subject Area: Elementary/Middle/High (Cross-curricular)

Standard/Objective:	Appropriate for any objective.
Activity:	Each student selects or is assigned an *energizing partner*, another student in the classroom who sits at a distance. Both students are provided with opportunities to stand and meet with one another to discuss any assigned task such as

WHY: RESEARCH RATIONALE

Because humans are mobile throughout life, we need an intelligent cognitive system that can transform sensory input and imagination into appropriate motor output—to decide whether to move or to stay. (Sylwester, 1995)

Standing appears to provide a 5–15% greater flow of blood and oxygen to the brain, thereby creating more arousal of attention. (Jensen, 1995)

Specific types of movements can stimulate the release of the body's natural motivators, such as noradrenaline and dopamine, which wake up learners and help them feel good, maximize their energy levels, and improve their storage of information and retrieval. (Jensen, 2000)

Neuronal connections made through movement of the body help children develop the neuronal systems they will need when ready to read. (Hannaford, 1995)

In the report *Champions of Change,* seven national studies regarding the impact of movement and theater tell of first graders dancing through the prepositions or fourth graders learning the states and capitals by running from state to state on a playground map, all resulting in increased student achievement. (Fiske, 1999)

Movement provides an external stimulus to go along with the internal stimulus. (Markowitz & Jensen, 1999)

Two places in the brain, the basal ganglia and the cerebellum, were once believed to be only responsible for control of the way we move our muscles but now appear also to assist with coordinating our thought processes. (Markowitz & Jensen, 1999)

Having students stand up, walk, jump, and clap as they review, understand, or master material will strengthen their procedural memories. (Sprenger, 1999)

Movement provides a new spatial reference on the room—more locations for unique learning addresses in the brain. (Rizzolatti, Fadiga, Fogassi, & Gallese, 1997)

Movement involves more of a student's brain than does seatwork since movement accesses multiple memory systems. (Jensen, 2001)

reteaching a concept just taught by the teacher (Gregory & Chapman, 2002).

- Level/Subject Area: Elementary/Middle/High (Cross-curricular)

  Standard/Objective: Appropriate for any objective.

Activity:	Students stand if their answer to a specific question is yes and remain seated if the answer is no.
Adaptation:	Students make a thumbs-up signal if the answer is yes and a thumbs-down if the answer is no.

- Level/Subject Area: Elementary (Language Arts)

Standard/Objective:	Recognize initial consonant sounds.
Activity:	Using the children's book *A, My Name is Alice* by Jane Bayer (1984), have students jump rope as each verse is read by the teacher or recited by the students.

> For example,
> *B, My Name is Barbara*
> *And my husband's name is Bob.*
> *We come from Brazil*
> *And we sell balloons.*
> *Barbara is a BEAR.*
> *Bob is a BABOON.*

Adaptation:	Students can make up their own jump rope rhymes for different initial consonant sounds. They can then jump rope to their original rhymes.

- Level/Subject Area: Elementary (Mathematics)

Standard/Objective:	Add one-digit numbers.
Activity:	Use students to show one-digit addition by having them demonstrate problems. For example, for the problem 7+3 = 10, have seven students come to the front of the room and then add three more students to the original seven. All students can then count the total number of students standing.

- Level/Subject Area: Elementary (Language Arts)

Standard/Objective:	Distinguish between common and proper nouns.
Activity:	Read a list containing both common and proper nouns taken from

content covered in class. Students stand when a proper noun in named and remain seated when a common noun is named.

- Level/Subject Area: Middle/High (Science)

  | Standard/Objective: | Demonstrate an understanding of the structure and properties of matter. |

  Activity: Following a discussion of the properties of matter, students pretend to be the molecules in solids by standing rigidly packed together; in liquids, by moving around one another but not apart; and in gases, by moving almost independent of one another and far apart.

- Level/Subject Area: Elementary (Science)

  Standard/Objective: Demonstrate an understanding of the rotation of the planets and their revolution around the sun.

  Activity: Students work in groups of 10. One student pretends to be the sun and the other nine revolve around the sun and rotate on their axis simultaneously.

- Level/Subject Area: Elementary (Music)

  Standard/Objective: Identify the notes on the treble clef.

  Activity: Students sit in chairs that represent the lines (EGBDF) on the treble clef. Other students stand in spaces between the chairs and represent the spaces (FACE) on the treble clef. When a note is called out or played on an instrument, students stand if seated or squat, if standing, if their position on the scale corresponds to the note played.

REFLECTION

> How can I integrate Strategy 10: Movement into my lesson plans so that my students' brains are engaged?

Standard/Objective:_____

_____.

Activity:_____

_____.

Standard/Objective:_____

_____.

Activity:_____

_____.

Standard/Objective:_____

_____.

Activity:_____

_____.

Standard/Objective:_____

_____.

Activity:_____

_____.

Standard/Objective:_____

_____.

Activity:_____

_____.

Standard/Objective:_____

_____.

Activity:_____

_____.

Music, Rhythm, Rhyme, and Rap

WHAT: DEFINING THE STRATEGY

Let a familiar song come on the radio, one that you haven't heard for years. In no time at all you will be singing along. Walk into almost any classroom and find several students tapping out a rhythm on their desk. Even Mother Goose and Will Smith have one thing in common—the ability to assist old and young alike in retaining information via the strategies of rhyme and rap. Why do these situations occur? Probably because music, rhythm, rhyme, and rap are some of the most powerful strategies to use in helping students retain explicit content.

I have heard teachers complain because students don't seem to be able to memorize important concepts. Yet, those very same students walk down the hall singing the lyrics to every popular song, by memory of course. Whether students are singing, rhyming, or rapping the alphabet song or the quadratic equation, teachers can experience success if they know how to use these strategies to their advantage.

HOW: SAMPLE CLASSROOM ACTIVITIES

- Level/Subject Area: Elementary/Middle/High (Cross-curricular)

    Standard/Objective: Maximize instructional time and
                            minimize transition time.

WHY: RESEARCH RATIONALE

Music from the baroque period appears to increase both memory and test-taking skills which, more than likely, are the result of the relaxation of body and brain. (Rose, 1986)

Music is a powerful carrier of signals that activate emotion and long-term memory. (Webb & Webb, 1990)

There appears to be a high degree of correlation between how well children could read both standard and phonic material and how well they could discriminate musical pitch. (Lamb & Gregory, 1993)

Brain scans taken during musical performances show that virtually the entire cerebral cortex is active while musicians are playing. (Weinberger, 1998)

Music activates and synchronizes neural networks which increase the brain's ability to reason spatially, think creatively, and perform in generalized mathematics. (Jensen, 2001)

National SAT scores from 1990 through 1995 give credence to the theory that music and the arts together have a positive effect on mathematics and verbal skills. (College Board, 2000)

Music appears very valuable as an aid to memory. (Sprenger, 1999)

Eighth graders who had received private music lessons for two years, along with music instruction at school, scored significantly higher on the composite mathematics portion of the Iowa Test of Basic Skills. (Cheek & Smith, 1999)

Low socioeconomic eighth through twelfth graders who took music lessons increased not only their math scores but also their reading, history, geography, and even social skills (by as much as 40%) when compared to their peers who had no music instruction. (Catterall, Chapleau, & Iwanaga, 1999)

Playing music, singing, rapping, whistling, clapping, and analyzing sounds are all examples of classroom activities that address the musical multiple intelligence. (Silver, Strong, & Perini, 2000)

Research appears to support great increases in students' spatial reasoning and mathematical problem-solving abilities when those students took piano lessons and worked on mathematics software. (Covino, 2002)

Activity: Students listen to classical music (i.e., baroque) during transition times to minimize disruptions and ensure a smooth change of activity.

- Level/Subject Area: Elementary (Language Arts)

  Standard/Objective: Recognize rhyming words.

Activity: Read poetry (e.g., *Mother Goose Nursery Rhymes*) to students initially for enjoyment. Then reread the selection as students listen for and name the rhyming words.

- Level/Subject Area: Elementary/Middle/High (Cross-curricular)

Standard/Objective: Recall information taught following a minilecture.

Activity: Students march around the room to high-energy, fast-paced music. When the music stops, each student recalls one major concept covered in the minilecture and discusses it with a student standing in close proximity. The procedure is then repeated with another student and a second major concept.

- Level/Subject Area: Elementary/Middle/High (Cross-curricular)

Standard/Objective: Recall information taught during a review at the end of the class session.

Activity: Students listen to baroque music to facilitate memory while the teacher reviews content covered during the class period.

- Level/Subject Area: Elementary/Middle/High (Cross-curricular)

Standard/Objective: Demonstrate understanding of a concept taught or content read.

Activity: Students work in cooperative groups to create a rap or rhyme that symbolizes their understanding of a concept taught or content read.

- Level/Subject Area: Elementary/Middle/High (Cross-curricular)

Standard/Objective: Demonstrate understanding of a concept taught or content read.

Activity: Students work in cooperative groups to write a song that symbolizes their understanding of a concept taught or content read.

- Level/Subject Area: Elementary/Middle (Language Arts)

  Standard/Objective:

  Recognize the syllables in words, paying particular attention to the accented syllable.

  Activity:

  Students stand by their desks, make a fist with their dominant hand, and push their arm straight out one time for every syllable in a multisyllabic word read aloud. If the syllable is an accented syllable, students raise their arms toward the ceiling rather than straight out.

  Adaptation:

  Have students clap out the syllables in a multisyllabic word.

- Level/Subject Area: High School (Mathematics)

  Standard/Objective:

  Memorize the quadratic equation in order to use it to solve problems.

  Activity:

  Students sing the quadratic equation as follows:

  Quadratic Equation
  (to the tune of Frere Jacques)

  Negative B (Repeat)
  Plus and Minus Square Root (Repeat)
  B Square Minus Four A C (Repeat)
  All Over Two A (Repeat)

- Level/Subject Area: Elementary/Middle/High (Cross-curricular)

  Standard/Objective:

  Demonstrate understanding of a concept taught or content read.

  Activity:

  Students work in cooperative groups to write a cinquain that symbolizes their understanding of a concept taught or content read. The format of a cinquain is as follows: first line—one word, second line—two words, third line—three words, fourth line—four words, last line—one word. Example:

  Brain
  Social organism
  Thinking, linking, connecting
  Necessary for life itself
  Life

REFLECTION

> How can I integrate Strategy 11: Music/Rhythm/Rhyme/Rap into my lesson plans so that my students' brains are engaged?

Standard/Objective:_____

_____.

Activity:_____

_____.

Standard/Objective:_____

_____.

Activity:_____

_____.

Standard/Objective:_____

_____.

Activity:_____

_____.

Standard/Objective:_____

_____.

Activity:_____

_____.

Standard/Objective:_____

_____.

Activity:_____

_____.

Standard/Objective:_____

_____.

Activity:_____

_____.

Project-Based and Problem-Based Instruction

WHAT: DEFINING THE STRATEGY

Which came first—schools or brains? The question appears to have a simple answer. Of course human beings had brains long before the creation of organized schools. In fact, the fundamental purpose of the brain is not to acquire good grades in school but to help its owner simply survive. Neuroscientists are finding that those brain characteristics that enhanced survival have endured throughout the years while characteristics that didn't enhance survival have disappeared over time (Westwater & Wolfe, 2000).

Is it any wonder, then, that information that the brain determines is important is much more likely to be attended to, stored, and later retrieved than that which the brain decides is meaningless and of little consequence for survival (Westwater & Wolfe, 2000)? Take a minute to peruse your curriculum. How many of the skills you teach are truly survival skills? Even telling students' brains that they must know the information to score well on standardized tests is not enough to gain and keep their attention for many of the abstract and uninteresting concepts that must be taught.

What, then, is the answer? Researchers (Diamond & Hopson, 1998; Wolfe, 2001) are finding out that solving real-life problems or completing real-world projects places a learner's brain closer to the reason it exists in the first place. Therefore, information acquired when students are engaged in the strategy of project- and problem-based instruction appears to be long retained. I bet you can recall a class project you completed in school, even if it was many years ago. Do you have the same degree of recall for a worksheet?

WHY: RESEARCH RATIONALE

Projects integrate curriculum across disciplines so that students see connections and interrelationships. (Uchida, Cetron, & McKenzie, 1996)

Eighty undergraduates found that it was easier to retain information if they (1) applied the new knowledge or skill within two hours after learning it; (2) performed tasks in various situations using the new knowledge, and (3) received regular feedback regarding their performance. (Goodwin, Grimes, & Erickson, 1998)

The problems that teachers develop for students should as closely as possible approximate the situation in which a real artist, engineer, or other professional attacks the same problem. (Wiggins & McTighe, 1998)

Brain research is confirming what many teachers already know: When learning is linked to real-life experiences, students retain and apply information in meaningful ways. (Westwater & Wolfe, 2000)

Project-based and problem-based instruction link new information to previously stored information that enable students to realize that they already have some knowledge about the new topic and that the activity is relevant to their personal lives. (Westwater & Wolfe, 2000)

Many educators today are exploring problem-based instruction as one way to encourage active learning and discourage student passivity. (Silver et al., 2000)

Student involvement in a project appears to be a much better way to learn if the project relates directly to a clearly defined objective or standard. (Wolfe, 2001)

Projects enable students to plan their time, develop research skills, and become responsible, independent, and self-directed, as well as to think abstractly. (Gregory & Chapman, 2002)

While engaged in solving problems, students must generate and test hypotheses related to the varying solutions they propose. These activities result in divergent thinking and exploring possibilities. (Marzano, Pickering, & Pollack, 2001)

In the real world of work, projects and fields of work are replacing ongoing full-time jobs. (Sternberg & Grigorenko, 2000)

HOW: SAMPLE CLASSROOM ACTIVITIES

- Level/Subject Area: Elementary/Middle/High (Cross-curricular)

    Standard/Objective: Master multiple curricular objectives.

    Activity: Identify several objectives from multiple content areas. Create a real-life project for students that will address all of the chosen objectives. For example, a project in which students write and produce a news program could address multiple objectives in a real world, memorable context. Objectives for this project could include the following: researching major current or historical events to determine the stories to be included in the broadcast, writing news copy that is grammatically correct with a main idea sentence in each paragraph, or broadcasting the news using appropriate public speaking skills.

- Level/Subject Area: Middle/High (Social Studies/History)

Standard/Objective:	Recall major Civil War events.
Activity:	Following a study of the Civil War, students show what they have learned by creating a Civil War newspaper that will recount the major events. Newspapers could include the following: a name, slogan, cost, index, front page feature story, additional stories, advertisements, obituaries, and so on.

- Level/Subject Area: Elementary/Middle/High (Mathematics)

Standard/Objective:	Construct bar and line graphs.
Activity:	Students collect data by surveying classmates regarding a topic of interest such as the number of students who prefer hot dogs, hamburgers, pizza, or tacos. Students then make line and bar graphs to depict the preferences of classmates.

- Level/Subject Area: Elementary/Middle/High (Mathematics)

Standard/Objective:	Apply understanding of multiplying fractions.
Activity:	Construct a class cookbook. Students find recipes for their

favorite foods that have fractions of servings; for example, 2½ cups of flour, 2¼ cups of sugar, ¾ teaspoon of vanilla. Students then rewrite the recipe cutting it in half and then doubling and tripling it. Students can choose one version of the recipe to make for homework.

- Level/Subject Area: Elementary/Middle/High (Mathematics)

Standard/Objective:	Calculate percentages.
Activity:	Following discussion of the procedure for calculating percentages, students are given the batting averages of several of the nation's top baseball players. Students work individually or in cooperative groups to figure out how the batting averages were derived. Students will need to know the number of at bats the player has had and the number of times a hit was made versus a strikeout or a walk.

- Level/Subject Area: Middle/High (Science)

Standard/Objective:	Recall the parts of an animal cell.
Activity:	Students are given a homework assignment to make a pizza that displays their knowledge of the parts of the cell. Students decide what toppings will be used to replicate cell parts; that is, pepperoni could be the nucleus. On a designated day, students bring their pizzas to school and evaluate one another's based on a rubric they helped to develop. Following the evaluation, the class enjoys a *Cellabration!*

- Level/Subject Area: Middle/High (Mathematics)

Standard/Objective:	Build a budget.
Activity:	Students are given an allotted yearly income. Working in pairs or cooperative groups, students plan a

budget that allows for living expenditures such as housing, utilities, food, and car. Students research the average cost of each expenditure and build a realistic monthly and yearly budget.

- Level/Subject Area: Elementary/Middle/High (Cross-curricular)

Standard/Objective:	Use data to solve a real-world problem.
Activity:	Each cooperative group is given a real-world problem to solve, such as, *What can be done about the water shortage in Atlanta? How can we increase parental participation in this school?* Students collect data and work together to derive the best solution to the problem. Each group writes a paper and makes an oral presentation outlining its possible solution.

REFLECTION

How can I integrate Strategy 12: Project/Problem-based Instruction into my lesson plans so that my students' brains are engaged?

Standard/Objective:_____

_____.

Activity:_____

_____.

Standard/Objective:_____

_____.

Activity:_____

_____.

Standard/Objective:_____

_____.

Activity:_____

_____.

Standard/Objective:_____

_____.

Activity:_____

_____.

Standard/Objective:_____

_____.

Activity:_____

_____.

Standard/Objective:_____

_____.

Activity:_____

_____.

Strategy 13

Reciprocal Teaching and Cooperative Learning

WHAT: DEFINING THE STRATEGY

Very few tasks in the world of work are done in isolation. The U.S. Secretary's Commission on Achieving Necessary Skills (A SCANS Report for America 2000) lists interpersonal skills as one of eight essential workplace competencies (SCANS, 1991). Yet, if every task assigned in class is completed individually or even competitively, are students really being prepared for their future workplace? Reciprocal teaching and cooperative learning provide opportunities for students to work in pairs or in small groups as they teach and learn from one another. In fact, Alfie Kohn (1999) suggests that the act of learning itself, at its foundation, is a social rather than a solitary act. Intelligence, he relates, is best applied to what goes on between people rather than what goes on in a student's head.

Several basic elements distinguish cooperative learning from traditional group work. In cooperative learning teams, activities are structured so that each student is individually accountable for mastery of the content (individual accountability) but also concerned about the performance of all group members (positive interdependence). The group's membership is heterogeneous with shared responsibility for leadership roles and group tasks. If necessary, the appropriate social skills for effective group functioning are taught and reinforced (Johnson, Johnson, Holubec, & Roy, 1984).

WHY: RESEARCH RATIONALE

We learn 90% of what we teach to others. (Society for Developmental Education, 1995)

A meta-analysis regarding social interdependence and achievement was conducted in which 122 different studies between 1921 and 1981 were reviewed. Results indicated that, regardless of the age level of the student or the subject matter taught, cooperative learning experiences tended to promote higher student achievement. (Johnson, Holubec, & Roy, 1984)

The following positive consequences come from peers' interactions with peers:

- Students learn attitudes, values, skills, and information unobtainable from adults
- Support, opportunities, and models for prosocial behavior are provided
- Students learn to view situations and problems from more than one perspective
- Students develop a frame of reference for perceiving themselves. (Johnson et al., 1984)

The dissolution of the traditional family, television models of anti-social, anticaring behaviors, and an unclear focus on values in the schools are all reasons why many students have little idea of how to behave in a social setting and why cooperative learning is so necessary. (Bellanca, 1991)

Students who work in cooperative groups learn to respect and value each other's different strengths, styles, and needs. (Bromley et al., 1995)

To prepare for work in the 21st century, opportunities must exist to enable students to work and learn in a team-like environment. (Uchida et al., 1996)

Freedom from the fear that shuts down the brain's ability to learn is a key component in the success of group learning. (Dougherty, 1997)

In a study of 40 middle school students, performance on weekly quizzes was significantly improved following reciprocal peer tutoring. (Malone & McLaughlin, 1997)

Math test scores of academically at-risk urban students were significantly higher following reciprocal peer tutoring. (Ginsburg-Block & Fantuzzo, 1997)

A student struggling to make sense of an idea may understand it better when it is explained by a peer (who only recently figured it out him- or herself) rather than by an adult. (Kohn, 1999)

Peer teaching gives students the opportunity to use two of the highest order thinking skills—synthesis and evaluation. (Sprenger, 1999)

Reciprocal peer learning strategies, begun in first grade, helped to prevent later reading failure. (Mathes, Grek, Howard, Babyak, & Allen, 1999)

Cooperative learning (in which readers work together to learn strategies within the context of reading) is one of the eight types of instruction with a scientific basis for improving comprehension. (Report of the National Reading Panel, 2000)

HOW: SAMPLE CLASSROOM ACTIVITIES

- Level/Subject Area: Elementary/Middle/High (Cross-curricular)

Standard/Objective:	Recall a concept taught or information presented.
Activity:	Ask each student to turn to a close partner (CP) and reexplain a concept just taught by the teacher, explain the directions of an assignment, or summarize the three most important points in the discussion.

- Level/Subject Area: Elementary/Middle/High (Cross-curricular)

Standard/Objective:	Read and comprehend a chapter, selection, or unit of study.
Activity:	*Jigsaw:* Students are divided into groups. Each student in the group reads and studies a different part of a chapter, selection, or unit of study and then teaches what he or she has learned to the other members of the group. Each then quizzes the group members until satisfied that everyone knows his or her part thoroughly (Johnson, Johnson, & Holubeck, 1990).

- Level/Subject Area: Elementary/Middle/High (Cross-curricular)

Standard/Objective:	Encourage participation in a cooperative group.

Activity: Students assume roles that expedite the group's functioning. These roles could include, but are not limited to, the following:

- Reporter—reports group findings to the class
- Recorder—writes down group notes or answers
- Time keeper—informs the group when half the time is gone and when one minute is left
- Encourager—facilitates participation by each student and praises students when they contribute
- Observer—informs students on how well they are practicing the social skills taught.

- Level/Subject Area: Elementary/Middle/High (Social Studies)

Standard/Objective: Describe ways in which language, stories, folktales, music, and artistic creations serve as expressions of culture.

Activity: Students are divided into six heterogeneous, cooperative groups with approximately five students in each group. Each group is assigned a particular culture to research. One student in each group researches the language, one the stories, one the folktales, one the music, and one the artistic creations of each of the assigned cultures. Each group provides both an oral presentation and a written report to the class regarding the culture studied. Design rubrics to assess performances and papers.

- Level/Subject Area: Elementary (Mathematics)

Standard/Objective: Recite the 1–5 multiplication tables.

Activity: *Drill Partners:* Students drill one another on the multiplication facts for several minutes each day until both partners know and can recite them all. Give bonus points on the multiplication test if both partners score above a predetermined percentage.

- Level/Subject Area: Elementary/Middle/High (Cross-curricular)

  Standard/Objective: Review assigned homework to check and clarify correct answers.

  Activity: Students work in pairs or small groups to compare answers on a homework assignment, discuss any disparities in answers, correct their papers, and provide a written explanation of why an answer might have been changed.

- Level/Subject Area: Elementary/Middle/High (Language Arts/English)

  Standard/Objective: Demonstrate understanding of a book read.

  Activity: *Book Report Pairs:* Students work in pairs to interview one another regarding a book that each read and then report on their partner's book to the class.

- Level/Subject Area: Middle/High (Language Arts/English/History)

  Standard/Objective: Demonstrate understanding of content read.

  Activity: Students work in small groups to write a play together about a time period recently studied. Group members then practice and perform the play for the class.

- Level/Subject Area: Elementary/Middle/High (Cross-curricular)

  Standard/Objective: Share cooperative group information with other students.

  Activity: Following the completion of a cooperative group activity, each group appoints a *roving reporter* whose job is to travel in a clockwise fashion to other groups and report the results of the original group's work.

REFLECTION

How can I integrate Strategy 13: Reciprocal Teaching/Cooperative Learning into my lesson plans so that my students' brains are engaged?

Standard/Objective:_____

_____.

Activity:_____

_____.

Standard/Objective:_____

_____.

Activity:_____

_____.

Standard/Objective:_____

_____.

Activity:_____

_____.

Standard/Objective:_____

_____.

Activity:_____

_____.

Standard/Objective:_____

_____.

Activity:_____

_____.

Standard/Objective:_____

_____.

Activity:_____

_____.

Role Plays, Drama, Pantomimes, and Charades

WHAT: DEFINING THE STRATEGY

Have you ever been to a party where the major entertainment was a very involved game of charades? If so, you will understand the overwhelming motivation inherent in the strategy of role play.

Semantic memory is one of the weakest memory pathways in the brain. This is why it is possible to cram for an exam and not remember any of the information once the exam is over. Therefore, an instructional strategy such as role play becomes increasingly important since it takes semantic information (i.e., memory for words, facts, and numbers), links it with movement, and places the information in more than one memory pathway. This cognitive–motor link is absolutely essential for retention of information.

Watch difficult concepts become easy to understand when students are actively engaged in *becoming* the concept being taught. For example, elementary students understand the rotation and revolution of the planets as nine children move in circular orbits around one child who has been designated as the sun. High school students comprehend properties of matter as they role play the action of molecules in solids, liquids, and gases.

HOW: SAMPLE CLASSROOM ACTIVITIES

- Level/Subject Area: Elementary/Middle/High (History)

    Standard/Objective: Recall the details of a major historical event.

WHY: RESEARCH RATIONALE

Role play affords students the opportunity to reach social, artistic, emotional, and academic goals. (Bandura, 1986; Brophy, 1987)

The use of role play makes learning more enjoyable, gives learners more choice and creativity, and results in little pressure from evaluation. (Jensen, 1995)

Emotional memories can be retrieved through performance. (Sprenger, 1999)

In a Chicago elementary school in which 84% of the students come from families in poverty and 30% do not speak English, once a strong dramatic arts program was implemented, the percentage of students reading at grade level increased from 38% to 60% and the percentage doing math at or above grade level increased from 49% to 68%. (Leroux & Grossman, 1999)

Those students with four or more years in drama study scored 44 points higher, and those with acting or production experience scored 53 points higher, on 1999 averaged mathematics and verbal college entrance exams than did those students with nondramatic experiences. (College Board, 2000)

Role play provides students with the opportunity to organize information, create or re-create meaningful situations, and use their verbal and interpersonal skills. (Gregory & Chapman, 2002)

Role-playing activities promote language development and help instill confidence in all students, particularly those who are not yet language proficient. (Vogt, 2000)

Role play and simulations, such as mock trials, are effective techniques for positively transferring new knowledge and skills from present to future application. (Jensen, 2000)

Dramatic arts can assist in the development of a child's emotional intelligence since these arts encourage students to manage feelings, communicate verbally and nonverbally, delay gratification, problem-solve, and resolve conflicts. (Jensen, 2001)

Simulations increase meaning, are highly motivating, and facilitate transfer of knowledge. (Wolfe, 2001)

Role plays increase the opportunity for understanding and retaining information since key concepts are put in the context of the learning situation. (Gregory & Chapman, 2002)

Activity: Following a lesson on a major historical event such as the first Thanksgiving or the signing of the Declaration of Independence, students create a dramatic presentation of the event, incorporating the major characters and details in sequential order.

- Level/Subject Area: Elementary (Language Arts)

  Standard/Objective: Recognize the appropriate use of punctuation.

  Activity: As students read a passage silently, they actually "walk" the punctuation—pausing for a comma, stopping for a period, shrugging their shoulders for a question mark, and jumping for an exclamation point (Wolfe, 2001).

- Level/Subject Area: Middle/High (History/Civics)

  Standard/Objective: Understand the judicial process.

  Activity: Following a discussion of the judicial system, students establish a peer court in which they try a classmate or a historical figure for a predetermined offense. Roles of judge, jury, prosecuting attorney, and defense attorney are assigned and carried out by members of the class.

- Level/Subject Area: Elementary/Middle/High (Cross-curricular)

  Standard/Objective: Determine point of view.

  Activity: Students create and present a commercial espousing a particular point of view or advertising a particular concept taught, such as saving the rainforest.

- Level/Subject Area: Elementary/Middle/High (Language Arts/English)

  Standard/Objective: Recognize story plot or sequence.

  Activity: Students act out selected scenes from stories or novels read.

- Level/Subject Area: Elementary/Middle (Language Arts)

    Standard/Objective: Recognize the function of a verb as one of the eight parts of speech.

    Activity: Students are given verbs to act out while classmates try to guess the verb.

- Level/Subject Area: Elementary/Middle/High (Cross-curricular)

    Standard/Objective: Review a concept previously taught.

    Activity: Each student is given a card containing the name of a concept previously taught. Students take turns pantomiming the assigned concept as the class attempts to guess the name of the concept.

REFLECTION

How can I integrate Strategy 14: Roleplay/Drama/Pantomime/Charades into my lesson plans so that my students' brains are engaged?

Standard/Objective:_____

_____.

Activity:_____

_____.

Standard/Objective:_____

_____.

Activity:_____

_____.

Standard/Objective:_____

_____.

Activity:_____

_____.

Standard/Objective:_____

_____.

Activity:_____

_____.

Standard/Objective:_____

_____.

Activity:_____

_____.

Standard/Objective:_____

_____.

Activity:_____

_____.

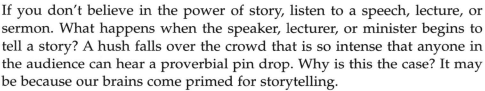

Strategy 15

Storytelling

WHAT: DEFINING THE STRATEGY

If you don't believe in the power of story, listen to a speech, lecture, or sermon. What happens when the speaker, lecturer, or minister begins to tell a story? A hush falls over the crowd that is so intense that anyone in the audience can hear a proverbial pin drop. Why is this the case? It may be because our brains come primed for storytelling.

Teachers have always known about the reaction of the brain and body when an interesting story is read or told in a reading or language arts class. However, a changing paradigm for the use of story is cross-curricular. Even the steps in long division can be mastered easily when those steps are organized into a story format. If that story is emotional, dramatic, or incorporates the strategies of metaphor or humor, its recall value increased.

As a former reading specialist, I often taught comprehension skills or strategies from a worksheet. I could not understand why my students could apply the skill within the context of the worksheet, such as bubbling, circling, or underlining the main idea, but could not apply the skill within the context of an actual longer poem or story. Knowing what I now know about memory pathways, it makes more sense that the lesson should begin with the same context in which I expect my students to apply the skill, the context of story.

HOW: SAMPLE CLASSROOM ACTIVITIES

- Level/Subject Area: Elementary/Middle/High (Cross-curricular)

Standard/Objective:	Comprehend the steps in a multistep process or events that happen in sequential order.
Activity:	Create a story to help students recall the steps in a multistep process such

WHY: RESEARCH RATIONALE

Students who used *narrative chaining,* linking items to be remembered into a story framework, could recall more than 90% of a list of 120 unrelated words compared to a control group who remembered only 13%. (McGee & Wilson, 1984)

Storytelling is a wonderful way to access more than one memory lane. Putting semantic information into a story format allows a student to see not only the whole idea but the details as well since the brain processes both wholes and parts at the same time. (Caine & Caine, 1997)

Good storytelling engages young children intently in the learning process and stimulates their interest in reading. (Goetz & Sadowski, 1996)

Stories provide a script for us to tie information to in our memory. (Markowitz & Jensen, 1999)

Emotional memory can be addressed through the conflict or plot of a story. (Sprenger, 1999)

During storytelling, listening and reasoning skills are improved as children use the auditory and frontal lobes of the brain to follow the plot of the story. (Storm, 1999)

Storying or linking can be used to teach long lists of information that should be memorized in a specific order. The story links each item to the next, similar to the links in a chain. (Deporter et al., 1999)

Storytelling addresses Gardner's verbal-linguistic multiple intelligence, which involves sensitivity to the meaning and order of words. (Hoerr, 2000)

Listening to stories replete with imagery encourages children to enter an imaginary world engaging the right hemisphere of the brain. (Jensen, 2000)

Storytelling, following intense learning, allows the brain to relax and more easily retain the newly acquired material. (Jensen, 2000)

as the digestive system or the steps in long division. Tell or read the story to the class. Have students retell the story to one another.

- Level/Subject Area: Elementary/Middle/High (Cross-curricular)

    Standard/Objective: Comprehend the steps in a multistep process or events that happen in sequential order.

Activity: Students work in groups or individually to create stories that help them recall the steps in a multistep process or events in sequential order, such as the digestive system or the steps in a long division problem. Students share their original stories with one another.

- Level/Subject Area: Middle (Mathematics)

  Standard/Objective: Regroup like parts of an algebraic equation.

  Activity: Tell the Story of the Algebraic Equation below to help students understand how to solve algebraic equations. This story also incorporates the strategies of movement, role play, metaphor, and demonstration. Seven students hold cards that represent the numbers and signs in the algebraic equation $3y + 10 = 2y + 18$. $3y$ and $2y$ should be female students. Ten and 18 should be male students. The cards for 10 and $2y$ should have -10 and $-2y$ written on the backs. Students' role-play the story as it is read.

- Level/Subject Area: Elementary/Middle/High (Cross-curricular)

  Standard/Objective: Comprehend skills and strategies through the use of stories and poems in literature.

  Activity: Select literary works that contain numerous examples of language arts skills and strategies. While a few titles are listed below as examples, any story or poem that contains examples of the skill to be taught can be used. Read the story or poem aloud to the class initially for enjoyment. Reread the story pointing out examples of the skill or strategy to be taught. Have students look for other examples in this or another literary work.

- Level/Subject Area: Elementary/Middle/High (Cross-curricular)

Standard/Objective:	Recall information.
Activity:	Students work individually or in cooperative groups to use the *narrative-chaining* method by making up a story linking together unrelated terms, concepts, or words in a list.

- Level/Subject Area: Elementary/Middle/High Language Arts)

Standard/Objective:	Retell story events in sequential order.
Activity:	Following a read aloud or the silent reading of a story, students retell the story to a partner with story events in the correct sequential order.

- Stories Used to Teach Skills and Strategies

  The Important Book, Margaret Wise Brown (main idea, details)

  The Day Jimmy's Boa Ate the Wash, Trinka Hayes Noble (cause and effect)

  Thomas' Snowsuit, Robert Munsch (sequence of events)

  The Pain and the Great One, Judy Blume (point of view)

  The King Who Rained, Fred Gwynne (figurative language)

■ THE STORY OF THE ALGEBRAIC EQUATION

$$3y + 10 = 2y + 18$$

Strategies: Storytelling, Movement, Role Play, Metaphor, Demonstration

Once upon a time, there were two families that lived on either side of a busy street called *equal street.* Each family had two children (one teenage daughter and one younger son). One day the teenage daughters, 3y and 2y, made a date to go to the mall. However, there was a problem. Each daughter had been asked to babysit a younger brother. 3y had to babysit 10 and 2y had to babysit 18.

The girls desperately wanted to get together to go to the mall. Therefore, one daughter, 3y, suggested that she send her younger brother, 10, to cross equal street so that he could play with her friend's brother, 18. Now there was one peculiar thing about this particular town. Whenever anyone crossed equal street, they had to turn around and cross it backward. So younger brother 10 turned backward and crossed the street. The two boys were very happy because now they could play together.

There was only one problem. In order to really be all alone with no one to bother them, the brothers had to get rid of big sister 2y. Now that was all right with big sister 2y since she wanted to go to the mall with her friend 3y anyway. So, she said goodbye to her brother and crossed equal street, backward of course, and she and her friend 3y could be all alone to proceed to the mall. The girls had a wonderful time and so did the boys.

Once the girls returned from the mall, they were in a world of trouble since their parents had told them over and over again never to leave their younger brothers unattended. But you know as well as I do that for generations older sisters have always left younger brothers unattended. That's just the way the story goes!

REFLECTION

How can I integrate Strategy 15: Storytelling into my lesson plans so that my students' brains are engaged?

Standard/Objective:_____

_____.

Activity:_____

_____.

Standard/Objective:_____

_____.

Activity:_____

_____.

Standard/Objective:_____

_____.

Activity:_____

_____.

Standard/Objective:_____

_____.

Activity:_____

_____.

Standard/Objective:_____

_____.

Activity:_____

_____.

Standard/Objective:_____

_____.

Activity:_____

_____.

Strategy 16

Technology

WHAT: DEFINING THE STRATEGY

Visualize the following classroom facilitated by a technologically knowledgeable teacher who is preparing students for their world. In one corner of the classroom, a group of students is developing a PowerPoint presentation as a culminating activity to a chapter on the American Revolution. Several students are on the Internet locating information for a project in which they are creating a Web page for their class. Several students are completing letters they will e-mail to their pen pals in Australia. Another group is watching a distance learning telecast of a science experiment, which they will perform for the class next week.

Technological advances have revolutionized all aspects of our lives including how educators teach and students learn. The SCANS Report (1991) lists technology as one of the eight major competencies essential for success in the real world of work and yet many schools are not equipping students with the knowledge and skills necessary for successful transition from school to work. The strategy of technology is not an option but a necessity if students are to be prepared for present and future occupational success.

HOW: SAMPLE CLASSROOM ACTIVITIES

- Level/Subject Area: Elementary/Middle/High (Cross-curricular)

Standard/Objective:	Use a word processor to write a paper.
Activity:	Students use a word processing program such as Word to produce a paper on an assigned topic.

WHY: RESEARCH RATIONALE

Schools should equip students to understand that the computer is an information, computation, and communication device. (National Commission on Excellence in Education, 1983)

Beginning in the mid-1980s, students became more engaged in using the computer for more authentic tasks comparable to those employed by professionals in the real world. (Means et al., 1993)

Technology, one of eight essential workplace competencies, includes the ability to choose equipment, determine the appropriate application for the task, maintain equipment, and correct technological problems. (SCANS, 1991)

Computer technology and databases are crucial for actively engaging students in conducting research, accessing information, and using resources to problem-solve or answer questions. (Darling-Hammond, 1994)

Computers and all forms of technology must be fully integrated into the curriculum—NOW! (Uchida et al., 1996)

Students will need to be skilled not only in accessing the vast array of information available through advanced technology, but in processing it as well . . . to prepare students, schools must incorporate marketplace technologies. (Uchida et al., 1996)

Technology enriches the curriculum by providing additional sources of knowledge and supplementing the textbook with various forms of multimedia. (Dede, 1998)

A technologically-based curriculum tends to be more specific, complex, visual, interactive, and global. (Glatthorn & Jailall, 2000)

Computer technology can be used very effectively to assist in teaching vocabulary. (Report of the National Reading Panel, 2000)

In this age of teacher accountability, technology-rich schools are at a definite advantage. (Lieberman & Miller, 2000)

According to the 1996 National Assessment of Educational Progress (NAEP), computer usage for the purpose of simulation and application (which results in higher math scores) was more prevalent with 8th graders who were ineligible for free lunch than with those who qualified for free lunch. (Wenglinsky, 1998)

- Level/Subject Area: Elementary/Middle/High (Cross-curricular)

  | Standard/Objective: | Interpret charts and graphs. |

  | Activity: | Students use Excel to produce charts and graphs accompanying an assigned project. |

- Level/Subject Area: Elementary/Middle/High (Cross-curricular)

Standard/Objective:	Produce a report on an assigned topic.
Activity:	Students work in cooperative groups to produce a PowerPoint presentation, which will be shown to and evaluated by classmates.

- Level/Subject Area: Elementary/Middle/High (English/Language Arts)

Standard/Objective:	Apply the characteristics of letter writing.
Activity:	Students correspond with a pen pal in another part of the world via e-mail. Each e-mail sent will adhere to an appropriate form and be grammatically correct.

- Level/Subject Area: Elementary/Middle/High (Cross-curricular)

Standard/Objective:	Appropriate to any objective.
Activity:	Students view a distance learning telecast with appropriate follow-up activities that reinforce the information acquired.

- Level/Subject Area: Elementary/Middle/High (Cross-curricular)

Standard/Objective:	Complete a research report.
Activity:	Students access the Internet to locate information related to an assigned topic. Students list the Web sites accessed in the bibliography of the report and incorporate appropriate information in the body of the paper.

- Level/Subject Area: Elementary/Middle/High (Social Studies)

Standard/Objective:	Make decisions regarding real-world events.
Activity:	Students complete a simulation such as *Oregon Trail* on the computer to experience what life was actually like for settlers in the Old West.

REFLECTION

How can I integrate Strategy 16: Technology into my lesson plans so that my students' brains are engaged?

Standard/Objective:_____

_____.

Activity:_____

_____.

Standard/Objective:_____

_____.

Activity:_____

_____.

Standard/Objective:_____

_____.

Activity:_____

_____.

Standard/Objective:_____

_____.

Activity:_____

_____.

Standard/Objective:_____

_____.

Activity:_____

_____.

Standard/Objective:_____

_____.

Activity:_____

_____.

Visualization and Guided Imagery

WHAT: DEFINING THE STRATEGY

My daughter, Jennifer, was having a very difficult time remembering the definition of the word *scullery*. Knowing her fondness for visual images, I simply asked her to visualize a black and white tile kitchen floor. I asked her to imagine that in the middle of that floor lay a stark, white skull. Since a scullery room is adjacent to a kitchen, Jennifer immediately made the connection. That was seven years ago. If asked today, Jenny would still be able to tell you the definition of the word *scullery*. That is just how powerful visualization can be to memory.

The more absurd the visual image, the more memorable it is to the brain. For example, imagine a herd of hippopotamuses wearing mortarboards and strolling single-file through a gate on a college campus. This visualization practically ensures that students will remember the term hippocampus, the brain's *gateway* to long-term memory.

Sousa (1995) relates that one reason today's students have such a difficult time comprehending when they read is because, in today's visual world, students have little opportunity to use their imaginations. Good readers are consistently visualizing the scenes in a story as they read. Therefore, the strategy of visualization provides opportunities for students to use their imaginations to facilitate both vocabulary development and comprehension across the curriculum.

HOW: SAMPLE CLASSROOM ACTIVITIES

- Level/Subject Area: Elementary/Middle/High (Language Arts)

    Standard/Objective: Increase listening comprehension.

WHY: RESEARCH RATIONALE

The image is the greatest instrument of instruction. If the majority of classroom time was spent ensuring that the student was forming proper images, the instructor's work would be indefinitely facilitated. (Dewey, 1938)

College students' retention of Spanish vocabulary was increased from 28% to 88% when the students linked a word's sound to the image of a concrete English noun. (Atkinson & Raugh, 1975; Raugh & Atkinson, 1975)

In a series of studies, training young readers in visualization while reading enhanced comprehension and memory for text. (Gambrell & Bales, 1986)

Visualization is a key strategy used by proficient readers. (Pressley, Johnson, Symons, McGodirck, & Kurita, 1989)

Visualizing and generating images are both crucially dependent on the right and left hemispheres of the brain. (Posner & Raichle, 1994)

Students can be taught to locate images in their minds or be shown how to select appropriate images that facilitate learning and retention. (Sousa, 1995)

Everything is created twice—once in a person's mind and once in reality. Visualizing something organizes one's ability to accomplish it. (Covey, 1996)

Visualizing is a comprehension strategy that allows readers to make the words real, like playing a movie of the text inside your head. (Keene & Zimmerman, 1997)

Visualization improves recall and problem solving when used following the learning of a task and before and during the application of new tasks. (Antonietti, 1999)

The more colorful the imagery we encounter when we initially learn a task, the better able we are to use similar images when we are later asked to mentally recall the situation. (Jensen, 2000)

When a person visualizes an image, that person is reconstructing the neurological networks that were originally formed when the initial stimulus was experienced. (Siegel, 2000)

Spatial-temporal reasoning, the ability to transform abstract concepts into visual images, is crucial for comprehending mathematics and science concepts. (Shaw, 2000)

Visualizing with wordless books helps readers build meaning. Visualizing with text does exactly the same thing. (Harvey & Goudvis, 2000)

Activity: Students are asked to close their eyes and visualize the scene as a detailed, descriptive paragraph is read aloud. Students then describe their scenes to one another and compare them to the original text.

- Level/Subject Area: Elementary/Middle/High (Cross-curricular)

    Standard/Objective: Comprehend a passage read.

    Activity: As students read a novel or content-area passage, they visualize the scenes or events using each of their senses. They answer the following question: What do you see, hear, feel, touch, and taste as you visualize the passage you are reading?

- Level/Subject Area: Elementary/Middle/High (Cross-curricular)

    Standard/Objective: Expand reading vocabulary.

    Activity: Students work in groups or individually to create visual images that link a word to its definition. The more absurd the visual image, the easier it is for the brain to remember. Refer to the word *scullery* described in the first section of this chapter.

- Level/Subject Area: Elementary/Middle/High (Science)

    Standard/Objective: Follow sequential steps in completion of a lab.

    Activity: Students read through the sequence of steps in a lab they are getting ready to complete. They then visualize and provide an illustration for each step in the lab to facilitate their understanding of the lab procedures (Ogle, 2000).

- Level/Subject Area: Elementary/Middle/High (Cross-curricular)

    Standard/Objective: Comprehend text.

    Activity: Students visualize the key idea in a paragraph of text and then draw an image to represent the idea.

- Level/Subject Area: Middle/High (Biology)

  Standard/Objective: Comprehend the passage of red blood cells through the body.

  Activity: Students visualize themselves as red blood cells coursing through a body as you use guided imagery to describe the path the blood cell takes. Students imagine the possible salty taste, the warm temperature, the wetness, and so on that the blood cell experiences.

- Level/Subject Area: Elementary/Middle/High (Cross-curricular)

  Standard/Objective: Recall a concept just taught.

  Activity: Students are shown a math formula, vocabulary word, or science process on the board or an overhead. The actual visual is removed and students are asked to visualize the concept and write it from memory on their papers.

REFLECTION

> How can I integrate Strategy 17: Visualization/Guided Imagery into my lesson plans so that my students' brains are engaged?

Standard/Objective:_____

_____.

Activity:_____

_____.

Standard/Objective:_____

_____.

Activity:_____

_____.

Standard/Objective:_____

_____.

Activity:_____

_____.

Standard/Objective:_____

_____.

Activity:_____

_____.

Standard/Objective:_____

_____.

Activity:_____

_____.

Standard/Objective:_____

_____.

Activity:_____

_____.

Strategy 18

Visuals

WHAT: DEFINING THE STRATEGY

Nothing is truer than the statement, "A picture is worth a thousand words." Computers, video games, and television are all tools which project pictures or visual images on the retinas and the minds of today's students. We live in a very visual world, so it stands to reason that one of Tate's 20 strategies should capitalize on the one modality that many students use consistently and have developed extensively—the visual modality. Types of visuals include overheads, maps, graphs, charts, and other artifacts that clarify the learning.

Jensen (1995) relates that 98% of what the brain takes in comes in unconsciously and is not a result of direct instruction. Therefore, pictures and words on the walls and items around the room take on an exaggerated sense of importance to students' brains. When students can look up on the wall and see the letters of the alphabet, the eight parts of speech, the periodic table of elements, or the steps in long division day after day after day, learning is supported. Whether the teacher ever calls attention to the displayed items or not, the information still gets into students' brains and, after all, isn't that what we want?

HOW: SAMPLE CLASSROOM ACTIVITIES

- Level/Subject Area: Elementary/Middle/High (Cross-curricular)

    Standard/Objective: Appropriate for any objective.

    Activity: Facilitate lecture or discussion by
                             writing key words and phrases or
                             drawing pictures on the board or an
                             overhead projector to emphasize

WHY: RESEARCH RATIONALE

Studies appear to indicate that the brain's capacity for long-term memory of pictures is almost limitless. (Bahrick, Bahrick, & Wittlinger, 1976)

National elections have been decided by concrete, visual images that make a lasting impression. (Petty & Cacioppo, 1984)

Since 90% of the brain's sensory input comes from visual sources, it stands to reason that the most powerful influence on learners' behaviors is concrete, visual images. (Jensen, 1994)

When teachers create a distinctive image to make a concept easier to understand, it instantly makes a highly abstract subject like math easier for concrete thinkers to process. (Deporter et al., 1999)

Linking verbal and visual images increases students' ability to store and retrieve information. (Ogle, 2000)

Understanding is increased when teachers encourage students to link verbal notes with images and symbols that show patterns, sequence, or relationships. (Sousa, 2001)

Since the eyes hold nearly 70% of the body's sensory receptors, humans take in more information visually than through any of the other senses. (Wolfe, 2001)

Visual learners acquire information most easily when they can see or read it. They prefer illustrations, pictures, diagrams, maps, and charts. (Gregory & Chapman, 2002)

When students' attention shifts from the teacher, having relevant visuals on the wall will ensure that students are still looking at material related to the lesson. (Allen, 2002)

key points. For example, write the word *noun* and the words *person, place, thing, and idea* as you explain its definition or draw a picture of the heart as you explain its function.

- Level/Subject Area: Elementary/Middle/High (Cross-curricular)

    Standard/Objective: Appropriate for any objective.

    Activity: Bring in a picture or a real artifact that students can see to clarify a concept being taught. For example, bring in a live gloxinia as you teach the vocabulary word for this flowering plant, show a picture of the Great Wall of China as you teach about its history, or bring in a pizza to teach the concept of fractions.

- Level/Subject Area: Elementary/Middle/High (Cross-curricular)

    Standard/Objective: Appropriate for any objective.

    Activity: As you lecture, provide students with a visual by filling in a semantic map or an appropriate graphic organizer emphasizing the lecture's main ideas and key points. Place the map or organizer on the board or an overhead. (See Strategy 5, Graphic Organizers, Semantic Maps, and Word Webs, for specific examples.)

- Level/Subject Area: Elementary/Middle/High (Cross-curricular)

    Standard/Objective: Appropriate for any objective.

    Activity: Place visuals on the classroom bulletin boards and walls that introduce or reinforce concepts being taught. For example, put a visual of the eight parts of speech on the wall as they are taught or display the steps in the process of long division.

- Level/Subject Area: Elementary (Language Arts/Reading)

    Standard/Objective: Expand reading vocabulary.

    Activity: Categorize basic sight words or vocabulary words by placing them on the wall under the appropriate alphabet letter or by parts of speech as they are taught.

- Level/Subject Area: Elementary/Middle/High (History)

    Standard/Objective: Comprehend the sequence of historical events.

    Activity: During the course of the school year, add specific historical events to a timeline placed around the wall so that students can visually see the relationships between sequential events in history.

- Level/Subject Area: Elementary/Middle/High (Cross-curricular)

Standard/Objective:	Use advance organizers to increase comprehension.
Activity:	Prior to reading content-area texts, students survey and discuss any maps, charts, and graphs to facilitate comprehension.

REFLECTION

> How can I integrate Strategy 18: Visuals (Overheads, Maps, Graphs, Charts)
> into my lesson plans so that my students' brains are engaged?

Standard/Objective:_____

_____.

Activity:_____

_____.

Standard/Objective:_____

_____.

Activity:_____

_____.

Standard/Objective:_____

_____.

Activity:_____

_____.

Standard/Objective:_____

_____.

Activity:_____

_____.

Standard/Objective:_____

_____.

Activity:_____

_____.

Standard/Objective:_____

_____.

Activity:_____

_____.

Work Study and Apprenticeships

WHAT: DEFINING THE STRATEGY

Think back to when you finished high school. No doubt you can recall the names of many students in your senior class who did not have the grades or the SAT scores to place in the top 25th or even the 50th percentile of graduating seniors. However, fast forward to your 10-year class reunion. How many of these so-called nonachievers became extremely successful in the real world of work? Could it be that much of the knowledge and skill one acquires in school may have little relationship to the actual knowledge and skill required for success in real life? Could it be that for some occupations, on-the-job training may be infinitely more valuable than memorization and regurgitation of isolated facts, which seem to earn the A's in school?

Work study, apprenticeships, practicums, and internships may be instructional strategies that afford students the best of both worlds: exposure in school to a wide variety of experiences that help students' determine possible career choices and actual on-the-job work experiences that prepare students for success in the real world.

HOW: SAMPLE CLASSROOM ACTIVITIES

• Level/Subject Area: Elementary/Middle/High (Cross-curricular)

Standard/Objective:	Appropriate for any curricular objective.
Activity:	As students cover various curricular objectives, professionals who use the given skills or knowledge in their daily jobs are invited to present to the class. For example, as math

WHY: RESEARCH RATIONALE

Learning should be organized around the principles of cognitive apprenticeships which stress subject-specific content as well as the skills required to operate within the content. (Berryman & Bailey, 1992)

What is needed is a marriage between academic and vocational education, between applying your mind and talents in both the school and hands-on learning environments. (Chion-Kenney, 1992)

The goal of school-to-career initiatives should be to make the educational experience relevant and allow students to transition successfully to the world of work or higher education. (Thiers, 1995)

Schools must link with businesses that can share resources, expectations, and vision. (Uchida et al., 1996)

Businesses and others who hire graduates need to pay more attention to what students have studied and how they accomplish knowledge in the work setting. (Uchida et al., 1996)

Students and their parents must be given a choice of a system that integrates school-based and work-based learning; that spans high school and postsecondary studies, and is planned by educators, employers, and employees. (Southern Regional Education Board, 1999)

We create new neural networks and our strongest neural networks from our actual experiences, not from paper and pencil tasks. (Westwater & Wolfe, 2000)

Career academies—small secondary schools organized around a major industry—improve attendance, lower dropout rates, and encourage at-risk students to successfully complete rigorous academic courses. (Manpower Development Research Corporation, 2000)

Adolescents' schoolwork must carry them into the "dynamic life of their environments." (Brooks, 2002, p. 72)

Large gaps exist between the kind of performance needed for success in a business setting and the kind needed for success in school. Educated adults are often unable to find a job or meet job expectations. (Sternberg & Grigorenko, 2000)

students study types of angles, an architect demonstrates to students ways in which angles play a part in building bridges.

- Level/Subject Area: Middle/High (Cross-curricular)

    Standard/Objective: Appropriate for any curricular objective.

Activity:
Students perform service learning projects for the school and community. Service learning engages students in providing a service while simultaneously mastering a curricular objective. For example, students create a butterfly garden in the courtyard of the school as a public service. As they create the garden and write about the process, students become engaged in numerous math, science, and English curricular objectives.

- Level/Subject Area: Middle/High (Cross-curricular)

Standard/Objective:
Appropriate for any curricular objective.

Activity:
Students partner with local businesses to participate in internships either during the school year or during the summer months in an effort to experience firsthand the knowledge and skills essential for success in the workplace.

- Level/Subject Area: Middle/High (Cross-curricular)

Standard/Objective:
Appropriate for any curricular objective.

Activity:
Students participate in Schools to Work programs. Consult the Internet for specific details.

- Level/Subject Area: Elementary/Middle (Cross-curricular)

Standard/Objective:
Apply and integrate multiple math objectives.

Activity:
Students take turns serving as apprentices in the school store to develop the knowledge and skills necessary for successful entrepreneurship.

- Level/Subject Area: Elementary/Middle/High (Mathematics)

Standard/Objective:
Apply and integrate multiple math objectives while learning fiscal responsibility.

Activity: Under teacher direction, students
                             plan and operate a school bank in
                             which fellow students deposit
                             money. Through this real-world
                             experience, students master
                             concepts such as deposits,
                             withdrawals, interest rates,
                             percentages, and so on. Students
                             take turns serving as apprentices in
                             the banking business.

REFLECTION

How can I integrate Strategy 19: Work Study/Apprenticeships into my lesson plans so that my students 'brains are engaged?

Standard/Objective:_____

_____.

Activity:_____

_____.

Standard/Objective:_____

_____.

Activity:_____

_____.

Standard/Objective:_____

_____.

Activity:_____

_____.

Standard/Objective:_____

_____.

Activity:_____

_____.

Standard/Objective:_____

_____.

Activity:_____

_____.

Standard/Objective:_____

_____.

Activity:_____

_____.

Writing and Journals

WHAT: DEFINING THE STRATEGY

Have you ever written a list of groceries that you wanted to purchase at the store and then forgotten to take the list with you? Isn't it strange that you can still recall the majority of items on the list? Perhaps this is because writing helps to organize and store memories.

The writing process is critical to students' ultimate success in the workplace. The SCANS Report (1991) lists writing as one of the basic skills essential for success in the workplace of the 21st century. The National Council of Teachers of English also supports the importance of students' mastering both the mechanics of writing and the ability to write creatively.

When the word *writing* is mentioned, teachers often think only of the full completion of the writing process: prewriting, writing, proofreading, revising, and rewriting. However, *quik writes* enable students to use this crucial skill in a multitude of cross-curricular ways for short periods of time.

HOW: SAMPLE CLASSROOM ACTIVITIES

- Level/Subject Area: Elementary/Middle/High (Cross-curricular)

Standard/Objective:	Expand reading and writing vocabularies.
Activity:	As vocabulary is taught, students are engaged in *quik writes*, which require them to take only a few seconds and write a synonym or antonym for the vocabulary word being taught.

WHY: RESEARCH RATIONALE

Students must be involved in the total process of reading and writing and should read literature and write for various real-life purposes. (Au, 1994)

Students' future success in an information society depends on their abilities to become an attentive listener, an articulate speaker, a clear writer, and a critical reader. (Fogarty, 1997)

Students should be encouraged to talk and write about their ideas, to understand the underlying concepts being taught and to put those concepts into their own words. (Kohn, 1999)

Students must write creatively and scientifically assisted by both hardware and software tools to aid them in writing, editing, and rewriting. (Uchida et al., 1996)

For centuries, writing down an account of an experience in a journal, log, or diary has been seen as the best way to remember it in detail. (Markowitz & Jensen, 1999)

Writing short, concise statements during note-taking improves both short- and long-term memory by priming the brain to store and recall information for future use. (Hadwin, Kirby, & Woodhouse, 1999)

Writing journals, newspaper articles, editorials, essays, posters, or short stories are examples of ways to access emotional memories. (Sprenger, 1999)

Writing down what is presented, observed, or thought about assists the brain in organizing and making sense of very complicated, multifaceted pieces of information. (Jensen, 2000)

Teaching students to use writing to organize their ideas about what they are reading is a proven procedure that enhances comprehension for text. (Report of the National Reading Panel, 2000)

It is one thing for students to succeed in writing good essays when teachers tell them what to write about; it is another for students to come up with original ideas for stories. (Sternberg & Grigorenko, 2000)

Adaptation: As information is presented, students are continuously engaged by writing key words or phrases the teacher wants them to remember.

- Level/Subject Area: Elementary/Middle/High (Reading/ Language Arts)

  Standard/Objective: Comprehend a literary work.

Activity:

After the reading of a story or poem, students respond in writing in one of the following ways:

- Write another ending to the story.
- Using the book as a model, write an original story patterned after the author's style.
- Pretend to be a major character and respond in writing as to how you would have handled the situation differently.

- Level/Subject Area: Elementary/Middle/High (Cross-curricular)

Standard/Objective:

Appropriate for any objective.

Activity:

Students use *quik writes* and reinforce the writing process in all content areas. For example, write the three causes of the Civil War. You have two minutes. Write an essay describing the steps in the process of long division.

- Level/Subject Area: Elementary/Middle/High (English/Language Arts)

Standard/Objective:

Experience the writing process.

Activity:

Students carry a piece of writing through the following five stages of the writing process for publication in a class book:
- Prewriting—Students brainstorm a jot list of ideas regarding an original composition or related to an assigned topic.
- Writing—Students write a rough draft of the composition according to teacher guidelines.
- Editing—Students assess one another's writing according to a rubric developed by the class.

- Revising—Students revise their composition in light of feedback from the rubric.
- Final draft—Students produce a written or typed final draft that is ready for publication in the class book.

- Level/Subject Area: Elementary/Middle/High (English/Language Arts)

    Standard/Objective: Expand reading and writing vocabularies.

    Activity: Identify tired words that are overused in students' writing, such as *said, like, good,* and *pretty.* Students brainstorm a list of synonyms that give them alternative vocabulary words to make their writing more interesting and appealing. For example, for the word *said* the brainstormed list could include *replied, exclaimed, declared,* and *stated.* Students are then forbidden to use the tired words and must incorporate the new words appropriately into their writing.

- Level/Subject Area: Elementary/Middle/High (Cross-curricular)

    Standard/Objective: Write for a variety of purposes.

    Activity: Students are given many opportunities to write for a variety of real-world, cross-curricular reasons. Purposes for writing should include the following: to inform, to persuade, to express, to entertain.

- Level/Subject Area: Elementary/Middle/High (Cross-curricular)

    Standard/Objective: Appropriate for any objective.

    Activity: Students are given a variety of opportunities to express their ideas in writing. These could include but are not limited to graphic organizers, posters, scripts for plays, and book jackets.

- Level/Subject Area: Elementary/Middle/High (Cross-curricular)

Standard/Objective:	Provide opportunities for personal journal writing.
Activity:	Students are provided time daily to write in a personal journal regarding topics of choice including descriptions of incidents that have happened at home, personal reflections on class assignments, or feelings and emotions expressed. Journals are not graded and students can indicate whether or not they want the entry read by the teacher by either leaving the page unfolded if it is to be read or folding the page lengthwise if it is not to be read.

REFLECTION

> How can I integrate Strategy 20: Writing/Journals into my lesson plans so that my students' brains are engaged?

Standard/Objective:_____

_____.

Activity:_____

_____.

Standard/Objective:_____

_____.

Activity:_____

_____.

Standard/Objective:_____

_____.

Activity:_____

_____.

Standard/Objective:_____

_____.

Activity:_____

_____.

Standard/Objective:_____

_____.

Activity:_____

_____.

Standard/Objective:_____

_____.

Activity:_____

_____.

Bibliography

Aldridge, N. C. (1999). Enhancing children's memory through cognitive interviewing: An assessment technique for social work practice. *Child and Adolescent Social Work Journal, 16*(2), 101-126.

Alexopoulou, E., & Driver, R. (1996). Small-group discussion in physics: Peer interaction modes in pairs and fours. *Journal of Research in Science Teaching, 33*(10), 1099-1114.

Allen, R. H. (2002). *Impact teaching: Ideas and strategies for teachers to maximize student learning.* Boston: Allyn & Bacon.

Antonietti, A. (1999). Can students predict when imagery will allow them to discover the problem solution? *European Journal of Cognitive Psychology, 11*(3), 407-428.

Armstrong, T. (1994). *Multiple intelligences in the classroom* (pp. 65-85). Alexandria, VA: Association for Supervision and Curriculum Development.

Astington, J. (1998). Theory of mind goes to school. *Educational Leadership, 56*(3), 46-48.

Atkinson, R., & Raugh, M. R. (1975). An application of the mnemonic keyword method to the acquisition of a Russian vocabulary. *Journal of Experimental Psychology: Human Learning and Memory, 104,* 126-133.

Au, K. (1994). Issue. *ASCD Update, 36*(5), 7.

Bahrick, H. P., Bahrick, P. O., & Wittlinger, R. P. (1976). Fifty years of memory for names and faces: A cross-sectional approach. *Journal of Experimental Psychology: General, 104,* 54-75.

Bandura, A. (1986). *Social foundations of thought and action: A social cognitive theory.* Englewood Cliffs, NJ: Prentice Hall.

Bayer, J. (1984). *A, my name is Alice.* New York: Dial Books for Young Readers.

Bellanca, J. (1991). *Building a caring, cooperative classroom: A social skills primer.* Palatine, IL: Skylight.

Berliner, D. C. (1984). *The half-full glass: A review of research on teaching.* In P. L. Hosford (Ed.), *Using what we know about teaching.* Alexandria, VA: Association for Supervision and Curriculum Development.

Berryman, S. E., & Bailey, T. R. (1992). *The double helix of education and the economy.* New York: Institute on Education and the Economy, Columbia University Teachers College.

Beyers, J. (1998). The biology of human play. *Child Development, 69*(3), 599-600.

Bjorkland, D. F., & Brown, R. D. (1998). Physical play and cognitive development: Integrating activity, cognition, and education. *Child Development, 69*(3), 604-606.

Blume, J. (1974). *The pain and the great one.* New York: Dell.

Bromley, K., Irwin-De Vitis, L., & Modlo, M. (1995) *Graphic organizers: Visual strategies for active learning.* New York: Scholastic Professional.

Brooks, J. (2002). *Schooling for life.* Alexandria, VA: Association for Supervision and Curriculum Development.

Brophy, J. (1987). Socializing students' motivation to learn. In M. L. Maehr & D. A. Kleiber (Eds.), *Advances in motivation and achievement* (Vol. 3, pp. 181-210). Greenwich, CT: JAI.

Brown, M. W. (1949). *The important book.* New York: Harper Trophy.

Brownlie, F., & Silver, H. F. (1995, January). *Mind's eye.* Paper presented at the seminar Responding Thoughtfully to the Challenge of Diversity, Delta School District Conference Center, Delta, British Columbia, Canada.

Burgess, R. (2000). *Laughing lessons: 149 2/3 ways to make teaching and learning fun.* Minneapolis, MN: Free Spirit.

Buzan, T., & Buzan, B. (1994). *The mind map book.* New York: NAL-Dutton.

Caine, R. N., & Ojemann, G. A. (1997). *Education on the edge of possibility.* Alexandria, VA: Association for Supervision and Curriculum Development.

Caine, R. N., & Caine, G. (1994) *Making connections: Teaching and the human brain.* Menlo Park, CA: Addison-Wesley.

Calvin, W. (1996). *How brains think.* New York: Basic Books.

Cardoso, S. H. (2000). Our ancient laughing brain. Cerebrum: The Dana. *Forum on Brain Science, 2*(4).

Catterall, J. S., Chapleau, R., & Iwanaga, J. (1999). Involvement in the arts and human development: General involvement and intensive involvement in music and theatre arts. In E. Fiske (Ed.), *Champions of change: The impact of the arts on learning.* [Online report], Washington, DC: The Arts Education Partnership and the President's Committee on the Arts and the Humanities. Retrieved from www.artsedge.kennedy-center.org/champions/

Cheek, J. M., & Smith, L. R. (1999). Music training and mathematical achievement. *Adolescence, 34*(136), 759-761.

Chion-Kenney, L. (1992). *Hands and minds: Redefining success in vocational technical education.* Washington, DC: Education Writers Association and William T. Grant Foundation Commission on Youth and America's Future.

College Board. (2000). *The College Board: Preparing, inspiring, and connecting.* (Online). Retrieved from www.collegeboard.org/prof/

Covey, S. (1996). *The seven habits of highly effective people.* Salt Lake City, UT: Covey Leadership Center.

Covino, J. K. (2002). Mind matters. *District Administrator, 38*(2), 25-27.

Dale, E. (1969) *Audio-visual methods in teaching* (3rd ed.). New York: Holt, Rinehart and Winston.

Darling-Hammond, L. (1994). Interview with Linda Darling-Hammond. *Technos, 3*(2), 6-9.

Dede, C. (Ed.). (1998). Learning with technology. In *1998 ASCD yearbook.* Alexandria, VA: Association for Supervision and Curriculum Development.

Deporter, B., Reardon, M., & Singer-Nourie, S. (1999). *Quantum teaching: Orchestrating student success.* Boston: Allyn & Bacon.

Derks, P., Gardner, J., & Agarwal, R. (1998). Recall of innocent and tendentious humorous material. *International Journal of Humor Research, 11*(1), 5-19.

Dewey, J. (1934). *Art as experience.* New York: Minion Ballet.

Dewey, J. (1938). *Experience and education.* New York: Macmillan.

Diamond, M., & Hopson, J. (1998). *Magic trees of the mind.* New York: Dutton.

Dougherty, R. (1997). Grade/study-performance contracts, enhanced communication, cooperative learning, and student performance in undergraduate organic chemistry. *Journal of Chemical Education, 74*(6), 722-726.

Dunston, P. J. (1992). A critique of graphic organizer research. *Reading Research and Instruction, 31*(2), 57-65.

Fiske, E. (Ed.). (1999). *Champions of change: The impact of the arts on learning.* (Online report). Washington DC: The Arts Education Partnership and the President's Committee on the Arts and the Humanities. Retrieved from www.artsedge. kennedy-enter.org/champions/

Fogarty, R. (1997). *Brain compatible classrooms.* Arlington Heights, IL: Skylight.

Fulk, B. M., Lohman, D., & Belfiore, P. J. (1997). Effects of integrated picture mnemonics on the letter recognition and letter-sound acquistion of transitional first-grade students with special needs. *Learning Disability Quarterly, 20*(1), 33-42.

Gambrell, L., & Bales, R. (1986). Mental imagery and the comprehension-monitoring performance of fourth-and fifth-grade poor readers. *Reading Research Quarterly, 21*(4), 454-464.

Gardiner, M. (1996). Learning improved by arts training. *Scientific Correspondence in Nature, 381*(580), 284.

Gardner, H. (1983). *Frames of mind: The theory of multiple intelligences.* New York: Basic Books.

Ginsburg-Block, M., & Fantuzzo, J. (1997). Reciprocal peer tutoring: An analysis of teacher and student interactions as a function of Training and experience. *School Psychology Quarterly, 12*(2), 134-149.

Glasser, W. (1985). *Control theory.* New York: Harper Collins.

Glatthorn, A., & Jailall, J. (2000) Curriculum for the new millennium. In R. S. Brandt (Ed.), *Education in a new era.* Alexandria, VA: Association for Supervision and Curriculum Development.

Goetz, E., & Sadowski, M. (1996). *Empirical approaches to literature and aesthetics.* Norwood, NJ: Ablex.

Goodwin, J. E., Grimes, C. R., & Erickson, J. M. (1998). *Perception and motor skills, 87*(1), 147-151.

Gregory, G., & Chapman, C. (2002). *Differentiated instructional strategies: One size doesn't fit all.* Thousand Oaks, CA: Corwin Press.

Gwynne, F. (1970). *The king who rained.* New York: Half Moon Books.

Hadwin, A., Kirby, J., & Woodhouse, R. (1999). Individual differences in note-taking, summarization and learning from lectures. *Alberta Journal of Educational Research, 45*(1), 1-17.

Hannaford, C. (1995). *Smart moves: Why learning is not all in your head.* Arlington, VA: Great Oceans.

Harpaz, Y., & Lefstein, A. (2000). Communities of thinking. *Educational Leadership, 58*(3), 54-57.

Harvey, S., & Goudvis, A. (2000). *Strategies that work: Teaching comprehension to enhance learning.* York, ME. Sternhouse.

Hoerr, T. R. (2000). *Becoming a multiple intelligences school.* Alexandria, VA: Association for Supervision and Curriculum Development.

Jensen, E. (1994). *The learning brain.* San Diego, CA: Turning Point for Teachers.

Jensen, E. (1995). *Brain-based learning & teaching.* Del Mar, CA: The Brain Store.

Jensen, E. (1996). *Completing the puzzle: The brain-based approach.* Del Mar, CA. Turning Point Publishing.

Jensen, E. (2000). Moving with the brain in mind. *Educational Leadership, 58*(3), 34-37.

Jensen, E. (2001). *Arts with the brain in mind.* Alexandria, VA: Association for Supervision and Curriculum Development.

Jensen, E., & Dabney, M. (2000). *Learning smarter: The new science of teaching.* San Diego, CA: The Brain Store.

Jing, J., Yuan, C., & Liu, J. (1999, May). Study of human figure drawings in learning disabilities. *Chinese Mental Health Journal, 13*(3), 133-134.

Johnson, D. W., Johnson, R. T., & Holubec, E. J. (1990). *Cooperation in the classroom.* Edina, MN: Interaction Book.

Johnson, D., Johnson, R. T., Holubec, E. J., & Roy, P. (1984). *Circles of learning: Cooperation in the classroom.* Alexandria, VA: Association for Supervision and Curriculum Development.

Kagan, S. (1998). *Smartcard: Graphic organizers.* In S. Kagan (Ed.), *Cooperative learning.* San Juan Capistrano, CA: Resources for Teachers.

Keene, E., & Zimmerman, S. (1997). *Mosaic of thought: Teaching comprehension in a reader's workshop.* Portsmouth, NH: Heinemann.

Kohn, A. (1999). *The schools our children deserve: Moving beyond traditional classrooms and tougher standards.* Boston: Houghton Mifflin.

Krepel, W. J., & Duvall, C. R. (1981). *Field trips: A guide for planning and conducting educational experiences.* Washington, DC: National Education Association.

Lakoff, G., & Johnson, M. (1980). *Metaphors we live by.* Chicago: University of Chicago Press.

Lamb, S. J., & Gregory, A. H. (1993). The relationship between music and reading in beginning readers. *Educational Psychology, 13,* 19-26.

Leroux, C., & Grossman, R. (1999, October 21). Arts in the schools paint masterpiece: Higher scores. *Chicago Tribune,* p. A1.

Levin, M. E., & Levin, J. R. (1990). Scientific mnemonomies: Methods for maximizing more than memory. *American Educational Research Journal, 27,* 301-321.

Lieberman, A., & Miller, L. (2000). *Teaching and teacher development: A new synthesis for a new century.* In R. S. Brandt (Ed.), *Education in a new era.* Alexandria, VA: Association for Supervision and Curriculum Development.

Malone, R., & McLaughlin, T. (1997). The effects of reciprocal peer tutoring with a group contingency on quiz performance in vocabulary with 7th and 8th grade students. *Behavioral Interventions, 12*(1), 27-40.

Mandel, S. M. (1998). *Social studies in the cyberage: Applications with cooperative learning.* Arlington Heights, IL: Skylight.

Manpower Development Research Corporation. (2000). *Career academies' impacts on students' engagement and performance in high school.* New York: Author.

Markowitz, K., & Jensen, E. (1999). *The great memory book.* San Diego, CA: The Brain Store.

Marzano, R. J., Pickering, D. J., & Pollack, J. E. (2001). *Classroom instruction that works.* Alexandria, VA: Association for Supervision and Curriculum Development.

Mathes, P., Grek, M., Howard, J., Babyak, A., & Allen, S. (1999). Peer-assisted learning strategies for first-grade readers: A tool for preventing early reading failure. *Learning Disabilities Research and Practice, 14*(1), 50-60.

Maynard, J. (2002). Model questions and key words to use in developing questions. In *Teacher expectations and student achievement coordinator manual.* Downey, CA: Los Angeles County Office of Education.

McCarthy, B. (1990). Using the 4MAT system to bring learning styles to schools. *Educational Leadership, 48*(2), 31-37.

McGee, M. G., & Wilson, D. W. (1984). *Psychology: Science and education.* New York: West.

Means, B., Blando, J., Olson, K., Middleton, T., Morocco, C. C., Remz, A. R., & Zorfass, J. (1993) *Using technology to support education reform.* Washington, DC: U.S. Government Printing Office.

Millan, D. A. (1995). Field trips: Maximizing the experience. In B. Horwood (Ed.), *Experience and the curriculum.* Dubuque, IA: Kendall/Hunt.

Munsch, R. (1985). *Thomas' snowsuit.* Toronto, Canada: Annick Press.

National Commission on Excellence in Education. (1983). *A nation at risk: The imperative for education reform.* (1983) Washington, DC: U.S. Government Printing Office.

National Council of Teachers of Mathematics (Eds.). (1970). *Mathematics and humor.* Reston, VA: Author.

Noble, T. H. (1980). *The day Jimmy's boa ate the wash.* New York: Dial Press.

Ogle, D. M. (2000). Make it visual: A picture is worth a thousand words. In M. McLaughlin & M. Vogt (Eds.), *Creativity and innovation in content area teaching.* Norwood, MA: Christopher-Gordon.

Parry, T., & Gregory, G. (1998). *Designing brain compatible learning.* Arlington Heights, IL: Skylight.

Pert, C. (1997). *Molecules of emotion: Why you feel the way you feel.* New York: Scribner.

Petty, R. E., & Cacioppo, J. T. (1984). Motivational factors in consumer response advertisement. R. G. Green, W. W. Beatty, & R. M. Arkin (Eds.), *Human motivation: Physiological, behavioral, and social approaches* (pp. 418-454). Boston: Allyn & Bacon.

Pinkofsky, H. B., & Reeves, R. R. (1998). Mnemonics for DSM-IV substance-related disorders. *General Hospital Psychiatry, 206*, 368-370.

Posner, M., & Raichle, M. (1994). *Images of mind.* New York: Scientific American Library.

Pressley, M., Johnson, C. J., Symons, S., McGodirck, J. A., & Kurita, J. A. (1989). Strategies that improve children's memory and comprehension of text. *Elementary School Journal, 89*, 3-32.

Raugh, M. R., & Atkinson, R. C. (1975). A mnemonic method for learning a second-language vocabulary. *Journal of Educational Psychology, 67*, 1-16.

Redfield, D. L., & Rousseau, E. W. (1981) A meta-analysis of experimental research on teacher questioning behavior. *Review of Educational Research, 51*(2), 237-245.

Report of the National Reading Panel. (2000). *Teaching children to read.* Jessup, MD: National Institute for Literacy at EDPubs.

Rizzolatti, G., Fadiga, L., Fogassi, L., & Gallese, V. (1997). Enhance: The space around us. *Science, 277*(5323), 190-191.

Rose, C. (1986). *Accelerated learning.* New York: Dell.

Rudman, C. L. (1994). A review of the use and implementation of science field trips. *School Science and Mathematics, 94*(3), 138-141.

Secretary's Commission on Achieving Necessary Skills. (1991). *What work requires of schools: A SCANS report for America 2000.* Washington, DC: U.S. Department of Labor.

Shaw, G. (2000). *Keeping Mozart in mind.* San Diego, CA: Academic Press.

Siegel, D. J. (2000, January 18). *The developing mind.* Speech given at the Learning Brain Expo, San Diego, CA.

Silver, H., Strong, R., & Commander, J. (1998). *Tools for promoting active, in-depth learning.* Woodbridge, NJ: Thoughtful Education Press.

Silver, H., Strong, R., & Perini, M. (2000). *So each may learn: Integrating learning styles and multiple intelligences.* Alexandria, VA: Association for Supervision and Curriculum Development.

Society for Developmental Education. (1995). *Pyramid of learning.* Peterborough, NH: Author.

Sousa, D. (1995). *How the brain learns: A classroom teacher's guide.* Reston, VA: National Association of Secondary School Principals.

Sousa, D. (2001). *How the brain learns* (2nd ed.). Thousand Oaks, CA: Corwin Press.

Southern Regional Education Board. (1999). *New partnerships and a national network to improve high school education.* Atlanta: Author.

Sprenger, M. (1999). *Learning and memory: The brain in action.* Alexandria, VA: Association for Supervision and Curriculum Development.

Sternberg, R. J., & Grigorenko, E. L. (2000). *Teaching for successful intelligence: To increase student learning and achievement.* Arlington Heights, IL: Skylight.

Sturm, B. (1999). The enhanced imagination: Storytelling? Power to entrance listeners. *Storytelling, 2*(2).

Sylwester, R. (1995). *A celebration of neurons: An educator's guide to the brain.* Alexandria, VA: Association for Supervision and Curriculum Development.

Sylwester, R. (1997, February). The neurobiology of self-esteem and aggression. *Educational Leadership, 54,* 75-79.

Thiers, N. (Ed.). (1995). *Successful strategies: Building a school-to-careers system.* Alexandria, VA: American Vocational Association.

Uchida, M. C., Cetron, M., & McKenzie, F. (1996). *Preparing students for the 21st century.* Arlington, VA: American Association of School Administrators.

U.S. Department of Education. (1986). *What works.* Washington, DC: Author.

Vogt, M. (2000). Active learning: Dramatic play in the content areas. In *Creativity and innovation in content-area teaching.* Norwood, MA: Christopher-Gordon.

Webb, D., & Webb, T. (1990). *Accelerated learning with music.* Norcross, GA: Accelerated Learning Systems.

Weinberger, N. (1998). Creating creativity with music. *Musical Research Notes, 5*(2), 2.

Wenglinsky, H. (1998). *Does it compute? The relationship between educational technology and student achievement in mathematics.* Princeton, NJ: Educational Testing Service.

Westwater, A., & Wolfe, P. (2000). The brain-compatible curriculum. *Educational Leadership, 58*(3), 49-52.

Whitin, P., & Whitin, D. J. (1997). *Inquiry at the window: Pursuing the wonders of learners.* Portsmouth, NH: Heinemann Books.

Wiggins, G., & McTighe, J. (1998). *Understanding by design.* Alexandria, VA: Association for Supervision and Curriculum Development.

Wilson, F. (1999). *The hand: How its use shapes the brain, language, and human culture.* New York: Vintage Books.

Wolfe, P. (2001). *Brain matters: Translating research into classroom practice.* Alexandria, VA: Association for Supervision and Curriculum Development.

Index

**CORWIN
PRESS**

The Corwin Press logo—a raven striding across an open book—represents the happy union of courage and learning. We are a professional-level publisher of books and journals for K-12 educators, and we are committed to creating and providing resources that embody these qualities. Corwin's motto is "Success for All Learners."